Never a Stranger

From her past in Croatia and Russia,
to finding a son in Bhutan, to befriending women in Africa,
one woman's stories of travel, connection, and self-discovery.

Tania Romanov

Never a Stranger:
From her past in Croatia and Russia, to finding a son in Bhutan, to befriending women in Africa, one woman's stories of travel, connection, and self-discovery.
by Tania Romanov

Published by solificatio

2019 Trade Paperback Edition
Copyright © 2019 Tania Romanov Amochaev
All rights reserved.

"Beneath the Surface" and "Homeland" previously published as standalone e-books.

More, including color versions of photos in this book at:
taniaromanov.com

ISBN-10: 0-9977619-3-8
ISBN-13: 978-0-9977619-3-1

Praise for *Never a Stranger*

"Tania Romanov travels with an open heart, a perceptive eye, and profound compassion. Her stories will help orient you on your own traveler's path."

— Larry Habegger, Executive Editor, Travelers' Tales

"When I look at Tania's images, I want to stay with them for a very long time, and then return to them over and over. She creates an emotional space for people to feel safe and embraced. The photographs show a compassion and a love for people that is deeply honest and profoundly moving."

— Catherine Karnow, *National Geographic* photographer and author of *Vietnam: 25 Years of Documenting a Changing Country*

"All across the globe, Tania Romanov searches for what is hidden—back through centuries, across generations, behind facades, in deserts, on mountains, through roadblocks and around obstacles. What she finds sparkles with significance for her … and, through her evocative writing, for us."

—Erin Byrne, author of *Wings: Gifts of Art, Life and Travel in France*

"Born of refugees who were forced from their home countries, Tania Romanov has learned to claim a place in the world—not by setting down physical roots, but by setting roots in the hearts of the people she meets in her travels. This book is a tribute to the home we can find in each other."

—Christina Ammon, Deep Travel Workshops

"It was an honor working with Tania for *Hidden Compass*. Not only is she an explorer with a special gift for connecting with people across cultures, she also brings an artistry to storytelling. Whether you're reading one of her essays or contemplating one of her photographs, Tania's work is a delight. When the two combine, it is the greatest delight of all."

—Sivani Babu, *Hidden Compass* Co-Founder

CONTENTS

1	A Lifetime of Travel	1
2	Not a Stranger in Bhutan	5
3	Trieste: Where Memory Starts	25
4	Beneath the Surface	39
5	Homeland	55
6	Irresistible India	67
7	Two Nomads, Three Camels	83
8	Behind the Facade	91
9	Ma Ganga	101
10	Echoes of Okunoin	107
11	On the Beach	113
12	Passage in India	117
13	Angels and Demons	123
14	Tenakee Springs	127
15	San Francisco Storyteller	137
16	Laughing Eyes	143
17	Evaporating with the Mists	145
18	Into a Disappearing Deep	159
19	A Precious Gift	167
20	Cuba in Color	177
21	Kilo Karinga	187
22	Himba and Herero	199
23	Connecting and Clicking	203
24	Samburu Softening	215
25	Angry Ancestors	219

26	Early Morning Rain	229
27	Nirvana in a Cup	239
28	Seven O'Clock	243
29	Sevilla Farewell	249
30	Do You Remember Me?	253

1 INTRODUCTION: A LIFETIME OF TRAVEL

I hang from the final limb of a family tree of generations of unintentional travelers—exiles, refugees, displaced people. I know all too well that not all travel is voluntary and that not every ship is a cruise liner.

My maternal grandmother, Katarina Marinovich, was deported with four children to a camp in Hungary during World War I. Only two of her children survived. As a further consequence of that war, she was later forced out—with her husband and five children—from her home by Mussolini, the Fascist Italian dictator.

My paternal grandmother, Daria Romanov, traveled as a girl with her family, migratory workers in Russia. As an adult, again in the aftermath of World War I, she fled that country—with her husband and four children—when the Communists overran the village where at last she had found a seemingly permanent home. It was not her final flight.

My parents, who, as infants, participated in those

involuntary migrations, as adults had to flee their own home—their adopted country, Yugoslavia—in the aftermath of the next conflagration, World War II. Daria was part of that exile, as were my aunts and uncles.

My brother and I were also part of that hardship: five years spent worrying, fleeing, waiting in a refugee camp and, finally, traveling to America. That last journey, so highly desired by my parents, was one I was forced into kicking and screaming, for I had to leave my beloved campo refugee family behind. I thank God to this day that they forced me along.

My father traveled to three continents. In search of refuge. In search of a home. The trauma of those displacements guaranteed that Papa rarely traveled far from his adopted homeland and never returned to the lands that had expelled him. Once he reached his next haven, he didn't need to move.

I, on the other hand, was young enough to enjoy the exploration and remain almost unaware of the pain. My childhood was populated with people who arrived from refugee camps and war-torn countries. In my mind their stories were grand adventures.

When my husband, Harold, moved to California, he started meeting those people and participating in their rituals. He loved the Russian Easter midnight mass celebrations and the late-night partying afterwards. He loved stories of experiences in Shanghai and Harbin, Venezuela and Argentina, Australia and Canada. Indentured servitude in Canada was fascinating; fleeing Berlin with the Belgrade Ballet Company in World War II was gripping; foreign languages—as long as I translated—were exotic.

It was through his eyes that I finally understood my thirst for travel.

I travel because it touches something deep inside of me. Because it connects me to who I am. To who I was. To the world.

And because I can't imagine not traveling.

I carry almost no luggage and buy few souvenirs. If my parents could come to a new life with no money and just a few suitcases, surely I can make a relatively short voyage with two changes of clothes and a comfortable ATM limit?

Instead of clothes I take with me a lifetime of experiences, an unquenchable curiosity, and a willingness to talk to anyone I meet. What I bring back is a trove of new experiences, a connection to a place and its people, and new insights into myself.

In India, I learned that to Indians the way I mourned my husband was far less personal than their own custom of dropping cremated bodies into a river; in Japan, that my ancestors could find me in the oddest of circumstances. In Bhutan I found family, and in Namibia I learned to ease my fears of being trapped in my own past.

My first journey—involuntary—took place less than a year after my birth. While I don't remember the details, it's as if I've often relived that entire experience, because my parents and their friends talked about it all their lives. I grew up with stories of exile—stories of adventure.

My life is richer for those stories, and I hope yours will be enhanced by reading mine.

TANIA ROMANOV

2 NOT A STRANGER IN BHUTAN

A fierce banging interrupted my hard-won sleep. I fought off the noise, drugged with the pill I'd finally been unable to resist after long days of travel on Bhutan's rugged roads. But the pounding persisted. The door rattled on its hinges. Footsteps raced heavily on stairs and down hallways.

"Get up, Tania! Get up! Now!"

I staggered toward the sound of Tandin's shouting, fumbling with the light. The switch didn't work. I wrestled the door open onto an equally dark, empty hallway. Tandin stood before me, a giant form in the blackness, flashlight in hand.

"There's a fire! Grab something warm and wait here for me. We have to get out! I'll be right back."

He tore off down the hallway, banging on doors, shouting.

Terrified, I found my headlamp and grabbed my glasses. I threw on my black down jacket and pushed my feet into heavy trail shoes.

I could hear fire crackling. I smelled smoke.

Tandin ran back, encircled me with his arms, and pulled

me toward the stairs directly across from my room. Flames lit up the back window of the stairwell, our only path out. I resisted, but could see no other option. I had to act—and quickly.

It wasn't the first time Tandin and I had faced peril.

Fourteen years earlier, in 2000, my husband Harold and I trekked for twenty-three days through the mountains of Bhutan, a Buddhist kingdom deep in the Himalayas. An intense expedition, it included climbing several mountain passes above the 15,000-foot elevation range. Tandin was our guide, a young man on break from school in Darjeeling.

I loved the Himalayas. We were experienced trekkers, and I was in my element.

Modern life receded when we landed in this remote country. The people of Bhutan, by law, all still wore traditional dress, the women in long, narrow wool skirts, the men in *gohs*—robes wrapped to knee length—even on the trek. There were no high-rises, few factories, and no fast food.

But as we drove deeper into the countryside, I started noticing something discomfiting and odd, something that appeared glaringly out of place in this seemingly circumspect society.

Penises.

Could it really be?

Our vehicle pulled into the last town before the trek. From there, we walked through villages unreachable by car.

Even here, every house we passed had penises painted on them. And these were not small or subtle sketches. These were giant, golden, erect specimens, some pointing up, some facing down. The latter often had huge testicles on top, with glorious hairy crowns. Prayer flags and penises somehow cohabited seamlessly in this land of unlikely contrasts.

Finally, I couldn't hold back the question.

"Why are there penises painted on the side of that house?"

It felt odd, asking the young man accompanying us on a long trek through the wilderness about penises, a man who was modestly covered by a wool robe.

"Oh," he replied, nonplussed. "They come from the teachings of the so-called mad saint in the sixteenth century." He told me that it was common belief that the phallus symbol brought good luck and drove away evil spirits.

Eventually, as we continued our climb into the high Himalayas, all houses, even those with penises, disappeared. We now passed only the infrequent dark-gray tents of yak-herding families and their stubborn, independent beasts. The ponies that brought our gear from the lower elevations went back down to replenish their oxygen. Up here, only yaks had lungs truly adapted to the environment, and they now carried everything. It was a delicate dance, for yaks could not survive below 12,000 feet—the air was simply too rich for them—and ponies couldn't carry heavy weight above that elevation.

About a week into the trek, as dawn approached, I crawled to the front of our tent. The ground was white. Everything was white. Slowly, outside I discerned large lumpy animal shapes like fallen snowmen. Our yaks, those giant bovine beasts, were sleeping in the meadow. I was relieved. The yaks had escaped the previous evening, and their herders had been searching for them late into the darkness. Their breath billowed around them. I headed back to my sleeping bag to wait for the young porter who would soon appear with cups of instant coffee.

We were at the stage of the trek that I always love most. My daily world of business, the bustle of city life, cleaning and cooking, cars and traffic, all receded beyond consciousness. Here there was only the present.

Harold woke briefly. I snuggled against him instead of into my own bag, ensuring not an inch of space came between us. I wanted to memorize the feel of his body, intimately familiar after twenty years of marriage. I didn't know how many more such mornings we would have. The white wisps of our breath mingled in the tent as he drifted back to sleep and I listened to the quiet sounds of camp stirring to life around us.

Meanwhile, I was preoccupied by one question: was I walking out of here?

It wasn't just the snow that worried me.

Yesterday we had climbed for hours along increasingly steep trails. Ominous clouds gathered as we approached a pass that crested at almost 16,000 feet. It was too windy to rest at the top, so we immediately headed down a steep, narrow trail. My pace was strong, hiking poles in cadence with my stride, weight centered, breathing smooth. I had acclimated to the elevation and was past the headaches, sleeplessness, loss of appetite and general inertia that had plagued me the first few days. My confidence edged on cockiness: I was in my early fifties, and proud of the fact that I was stronger than I'd ever been.

Near the top every step was a challenge. But then the decline eased, and frightening cliff exposures faded into memory. I glanced back toward the pass, relieved to see our yak train following behind. That's when it happened.

My foot slipped out from under me.

Suddenly I was sliding on my back, then skidding to a halt.

No big deal, I thought. I'll get up, sweep the dirt off my rear, and continue.

No sooner did I try to get up, however, than I was back on my butt. Excruciating pain shot through my left leg.

"Are you OK?"

Harold caught up just in time to see my failed attempt to get back up.

"I'm sure it'll be fine," I said, putting my head between my knees and breathing deeply. "I just need a minute to recover." I desperately wanted it to be true.

But when I put my hand on my ankle, I flinched again from the pain.

"Take off your boot," Harold suggested, kneeling next to me. "Let me take a look."

The rest of the hikers joined us, concerned. My world was shrinking, focused on a small spot in my lower left leg. My ankle had already started swelling. Soon I could barely get it back into the boot. There was no way I was walking.

My mind kept going back and forth between pain and fear. The alternatives were few. The yaks were out of the question—I had seen their antics, the herders trying desperately to get them under control. Our single remaining pony was long gone, two thousand feet somewhere below us.

As I wondered what we could do, our young guide squatted beside me. Unlike the others supporting our team, who resembled a mix of the people of Nepal and China, Tandin was tall and large-boned. His features were chiseled onto a long narrow face, and he looked as if he could stride a Mongolian plain with an eagle on his arm. But his rugged face was comforting, exactly what I needed at the moment.

"I will carry you, Tania."

He spoke quietly, with a confidence I didn't expect in someone so young.

I looked around. No one had a better idea. The break had stretched out, and it was still a four-hour walk to camp. Harold helped me stand up and took my things. Tandin moved his daypack to his chest and prepared to lift me onto his back. He held one arm under my left knee so my ankle wouldn't bounce. Finally, he started off, down the mountain, every foot-plant landing firmly, as if we were in Central Park and not on the side of a Himalayan peak. I clung to him like a giant breathing backpack. At first each step was jarring, but either the Advil or exhaustion soon mellowed me out.

For the two hours it took to reach the base of the slope, Tandin entertained me with stories about his childhood. I don't remember the scenery—or much else—but I remember that Tandin played basketball with the crown prince—now king—of Bhutan. That he participated in archery contests. That his father had left when he was very young and remained estranged from the family, and his mother lived in the remote village where she was born, although the rest of the family had moved to the capital, Thimphu. And I learned all about Grandfather, the patriarch of his clan and a devout Buddhist. In Bhutan, Tandin explained, it is the husband who moves in with his wife's family, rather than the other way around, as in China and India. Grandfather had six daughters, and he had to provide housing for all their families.

After a long descent, we finally reached the horse. It had no saddle. There was no way for me to ride it.

Tandin carefully lowered me onto a large rock. I passed out. My choice was clear: Tandin would have to carry me for another two hours, all the way to our camp.

That evening in camp, my ankle had swollen far beyond the size of my boots. Our medicine kit consisted of Advil and arnica gel. I had never heard of the latter.

"It's a special healing cream, and it reduces swelling," said my friend Jean, as she sat on Harold's cot in our tent. "I never go anywhere without it. Can I put some on your ankle? I'm sure it will make it feel better."

The very thought of anyone touching my ankle was nearly unbearable. But Jean warmed her hands, spread the cream evenly on them, and then, as if coddling a newborn baby, gently caressed every inch from my toes to my knees.

She performed that ritual three times a day and, by the second evening, the swelling had reduced to nearly normal. I already believed arnica gel was a miracle medicine.

Just after dawn our second morning at camp, the porter arrived, calling "Hello sir!" as always.

That meant me, I knew. Everyone was "sir." In his usual flip-flops, he stood in the snow outside the tent and poured steaming-hot liquid into a banged-up metal cup, which, at that moment, was more exquisite to me than the finest China.

We had already spent an unplanned extra day here. Between two major mountain passes, we had no radio signal and no way to call for a helicopter. The nearest road was a many-days walk away, and we were less than halfway through one of the most challenging trips in Bhutan.

After the coffee, washing, and packing, Harold lifted me

out of the breakfast tent and helped me onto a rock. Jean gave me a final rub of arnica. I then put on a thick pair of socks and eased into my heavy leather boots. I tied the laces firmly enough to hold my foot steady. Harold and Jean each gripped me under an arm as I came to a standing position. Jean's husband Yves and the rest of the group stood in a broad circle. A lot was riding on that moment.

Slowly, I put weight onto my left foot, as everyone watched with bated breath. I was barely aware of them. All my concentration was on my thigh muscle, on carefully lowering my knee, on the toe of my boot touching the ground.

I screamed, obliterating the silence. Excruciating pain tore through my body. Tears streamed down my face. Harold and Jean held on tightly, afraid to jostle me. I stood on my good leg, desperate to do anything but give up.

As I looked at Yves, I remembered our first meeting a few months earlier. He was the organizer of the expedition, and he wanted to make sure Harold and I were prepared. Yves was tough. He had served in the French Foreign Legion in Algeria, and he suffered no wimps.

I had taken Harold helicopter skiing in Canada for his sixtieth birthday that January and fallen on the first run. He'd kept skiing while I was helicoptered out. My ACL was broken; it had required surgery and a minimum of six months to heal.

I had had to convince Yves that six months and two weeks after surgery I would be ready for this trek. I told him I was as tough as he was.

Now I had to prove it.

But there was a far more important reason for my desperate determination. Five years earlier, Harold had started fighting an aggressive prostate cancer that didn't disappear as it should have post surgery. He was given a two- or three-year life expectancy. I quit my job, and we started on all the adventures we didn't have time for while working and raising children. Harold was doing well presently, but the periodic treatments sapped his energy. It was no small miracle that he could even still do this rigorous hiking.

My ankle made us two cripples, not just one. I was as determined to continue for him as for myself, because we never knew how much longer he would be walking.

Instead of doing the rational thing, I breathed deeply, looked Harold in the eyes as he wiped my face with his hand, and said: "I can do this."

Harold turned to the others and asked for a moment alone. They walked away, no doubt considering contingency plans. We sat down. Harold caressed my hand, waiting until I was calm.

"You know we can figure something out," he said, "some way to get out of here."

"No, Harold, it's really OK. I can do this."

"Baby, are you thinking about me or yourself?"

I just looked at him, not even understanding the question. Without my realizing it, Harold and his illness and I had merged into a single unit. Something precious and unbreakable.

"I'll do it, sweetheart. Really."

That single first step, that moment of pain, had somehow expelled the unendurable. Or I had just understood and adapted to the challenge before me. I had always believed I had a high pain tolerance.

That belief was about to be tested.

I will never know how I did it—how I continued hiking on

a broken ankle—but I do know that for the next twenty days my only medication was Advil and the thrice-daily tender, almost ritualistic, application of arnica gel, a medicine I have never been without since.

We didn't just stroll. We were above fourteen thousand feet of elevation most of the time. We crossed three more high passes—all of them higher than the tallest mountain in the United States.

A cultural trait of the Bhutanese people is their inability to say anything negative. No matter how often we asked, the guides replied that the destination was "not too much farther," even though some days we hiked for more than fourteen hours. Our longest day ended in a blinding snowstorm; the next morning we woke to two feet of snow on the tents. Level surfaces did not exist in these mountains; we were either climbing or descending. Some of our fellow travelers came close to giving up, but I just persisted. Through it all, Tandin was never far from my side.

Some days after my fall, Harold and I sat alone on a boulder above the trail. The mountains glistened; we had just passed wild sheep clambering on the rocks. It was a moment that reminded us why we always pushed ourselves to the limit instead of sitting on a beach in a fancy resort. I leaned between his open knees, feeling the warmth of his chest, daydreaming until his words brought me back.

"Tania," he said, "we should have Tandin come to school in California, maybe live with us."

"Really?"

I paused. I had been thinking the same thing. After all these years together, that happened often.

"That sounds lovely," I said, "but do you think we can handle something like that? I thought we wanted to be free, you know, to do stuff..."

"Of course I still want that, but something in me also wants to do something for him. If it wasn't for Tandin..." his voice dropped off. "I don't know where we would be right now. Don't tell me you haven't been thinking the same thing."

He knew me too well. Perhaps he also saw illness limiting his days, his ability to share.

"Do you think you'd have the energy to work with him?"

"Even if I don't, it would still be a great opportunity. Besides, you've always had enough drive for both of us."

It was an old joke between us, but I suspected he was right. Like many things that can't be explained, this idea just felt natural to us. We let it evolve.

Near the end of the trek, Tandin led us through remote villages that might as well have been in the Middle Ages. Behind sensuously curved, golden fields of rice, rose forests capped by snow-covered peaks. In one field, a young woman stood atop a large pile of rice sheaves. Her round face was topped with a cap of black hair. She wore a long skirt with a rich violet print and a bold brocade jacket over a green blouse. She stared, curious. Tandin came into view and—as everyone always did upon meeting him—she smiled. The villagers gathered around him, smiling, laughing, and joking. He played with the children, flirted with the young women, teased the grandmothers. Even the dogs came to play with him.

"Tandin, do you know these people?" Harold asked, mystified.

"Oh, no." He gave a delicate nod, so characteristic of his people. "I've never been here before."

But he had been in similar places. Thoughts of his mother's farm and village were often on Tandin's mind as we walked through this final part of the trek.

"You cannot imagine how hard these people work to achieve this day of harvest," he said. "Everything is done manually: the clearing of the terraces, the plowing, the planting, the tending to the fields. And the continual worry about the pigs."

I had stopped to look at a small raised platform over one of the terraces.

"That's where children spend nights," he said, "trying to stay awake, hoping to scare the pigs away."

"Really?" Harold and I were used to neighbors who shot wild pigs, not children who were planted to scare them. But the Buddhist tradition of non-violence made it difficult to deal with the pigs, even though they ruined twenty-five to thirty percent of the crop each year.

"For a while we tried putting firecrackers on a string, so we wouldn't have to stay up all night," said Tandin. "But the pigs quickly figured out there was noise but no real danger and learned to ignore them."

As he talked, my mental image shifted. I thought of the hand-powered flashlight Tandin had in camp, whose quiet clattering reminded us that batteries were both expensive and hard to dispose of in this still-unpolluted land. I became aware of the difference between our visions of the scene surrounding us. To me it was a glorious glimpse into a life that had disappeared in most of the world, buried under layers of technological evolution. It was easy to romanticize the artful terracing, the black oxen pulling hand-carved wooden plows, the grain flying and glowing in the sunlight as women stood on mats and winnowed rice, using large, round woven-straw trays.

As seductive as a seventeenth century Vermeer canvas brought to life, it touched the Russian-peasant roots deep inside of me. I was awed and grateful. Grateful to be here at this moment, wanting to sink into the rice at my feet and absorb the experience into the depths of my being. And—on a level I could not be proud of—grateful that I was but passing through; that when winter came and it got cold and dark in this deep valley with no amenities, I would be back in my life of luxury and ease.

"Tandin, is this what your village looked like?" I asked.

"Oh, yes."

"Did you spend nights on these pig-watching platforms?"

"Oh, yes." He nodded, then paused. "When I would come home from my school in Thimphu, I would have to do this."

He paused again, and a memory that wasn't as enchanting as the scene around us played briefly over his features. "But it is better for someone more serious, who is not so tired from school, who wouldn't fall asleep, to be the one guarding the fields."

I smiled. He grinned sheepishly.

Tandin had an intimate knowledge of the life in this village, but he had already started putting distance between himself and it. I envisioned him around the fire the previous night, when we'd asked if he would sing for us. Instead of some romantic Bhutanese ballad, we were surprised to hear Eric Clapton. The outside world was seeping into Tandin; it was a spigot that would be hard to close.

Now he grew serious.

"As hard as these people work, they will give away much of this rice, and very quickly," he said.

"What do you mean?" I asked.

"They will finish the harvest, and then it will be time for their *putscha*. To gain face with their neighbors, they will make it as grand a feast as possible and send everyone home heavily laden with gifts. When it is over, much of what they have worked for all year will be gone. They will have to subsist on what is left for the rest of the year."

Clearly he was troubled by this practice. He had told us that farmers showed their wealth by leaving the rice stacks in the fields a long time—to advertise their lack of an imminent need for it, even though it could start rotting. Wealthier farmers served and ate old rice, left from previous harvests, rather than the fresh new grains, to boast of abundance.

We had our own ways of showing wealth and status in America, our own issues of "keeping up with the Joneses." And Harold and I realized that if Tandin came to California, our customs would seem as strange to him as eating old rice to prove superiority was to us. We envisioned translating American behavior for him, just as he had helped open up Bhutan for us.

Our conversations, after all, were two-way streets. Tandin absorbed information about us, too, as we shared more about ourselves. Harold and I had both been successful computer business executives. To Tandin, our freedom to do what we wanted spoke of the benefit of studying computers and technology. Before we even knew what happened, he told us that he, too, wanted to study computers.

We felt Tandin's skills perhaps lay elsewhere, in his ability to captivate and lead; but we were reluctant to discourage him in his newfound mission.

"Tandin," Harold asked one day, as we walked through a forest whose trees had orchids growing from their trunks, "what would you think of going to college in America?"

I had been hanging back, entranced. Now we all paused

and looked at each other. We knew it was an important moment.

"Oh... That would be amazing, but I do not believe I would qualify," he replied, each word carefully considered. "My grades were not so great, and my test scores are not high. And I could not afford it without a scholarship."

But we could see the raw desire in his eyes.

By the time we again reached Thimphu, we were anxious to meet Tandin's grandfather, whom we'd heard so much about. We wanted his blessing on our idea.

Grandfather was a man of dignity and strength, of calm. Slight of stature, he was slim and straight as the bamboo arrows he, too, had shot in his youth. His wrinkles were like the bark of a tree, but his eyes sparkled and he smiled easily. His gnarled fingers never stopped moving over his prayer beads.

Grandfather didn't say much, but he listened carefully. Even seated, Harold towered over everyone else in the room, but for some reason he seemed the supplicant as he explained our idea.

Grandfather eventually spoke. Tandin translated.

"I understand how my family might benefit from your offer. I understand how Tandin might benefit."

Here Tandin paused, as if concerned about what came next. Finally, he looked at Harold and me, then continued.

"But how do you benefit from bringing my grandson to America and sending him to college?"

Everyone now stared at Harold—Tandin with trepidation, Grandfather inscrutably, the others with curiosity. We sat on floor mats, and yak-butter tea sat mostly untouched—by me, at least—in simple pottery cups before us. Harold, while fighting for his life since the cancer diagnosis, had developed a wisdom that could still surprise me.

"I am a relatively new student of Buddhism," he began, "but I like what it teaches about releasing goodness into the universe and seeing how it circles, perhaps returning when you don't expect it."

Grandfather's face broke into a rare grin. I knew Harold and I had just been accepted into his extended family.

Tandin and Grandfather exchanged a few words. Then Tandin turned to us, chagrined.

"Grandfather wants you to know I have not always been a model student. Or the most obedient son."

"Tell him we already figured that out."

Tandin's relief was obvious. We agreed to set up an email account for him, and he would use the computer at a café in town to communicate with us.

We left Bhutan believing we would soon have a student in our household again.

A lot changed in the aftermath of the comparatively innocent days when we'd hiked the Himalayas with Tandin. The 9/11 Twin Tower bombing in New York eliminated any possibility of the United States granting Tandin a visa to study in California. A scholar heading for Stanford or Harvard, maybe. A young man headed for Santa Rosa Junior College, no way. After extensive letter exchanges with congressmen and consulates and colleges, we realized we had hit a dead-end.

While we struggled to come up with an alternative, Tandin was accepted to a college in Bangkok. After consultation with his family, we agreed to send him there to study computer science.

At first he sent regular letters and reports; then, in the second year, communication dropped off. Tandin was half the world away, so it was hard to feel personally involved, to help. Less than eighteen months into it, we learned he had failed out of the program. He was simply unsuited for it. But we heard nothing from him.

Were we pouring money down a rathole or supporting a promising young man, someone struggling but worth our continued commitment? Was Tandin likely to stay connected with two people in far-off America? Or had he already disappeared, just another undocumented immigrant whom we had inadvertently launched into the world?

It was fortunate that Tandin reminded us of our own son. Brad had struggled through school, yet eventually earned two master's degrees. Whenever he ran into problems, he retreated, became hard to communicate with. We knew this scenario intimately. Rather than cut our risks, we held onto our faith.

When Tandin realized that we weren't giving up even though he had failed, he found another program. It would let him work year-round and finish in three years.

"You won't regret this, I promise you," he emailed.

In spite of restarting at a new school, in just over four years, Tandin graduated from Bangkok University with a bachelor's degree in Hospitality and Tourism Management. By then he had also met and fallen in love with Chhimi, a fellow student from Bhutan. Although Harold wasn't well enough to attend the graduation ceremony, he always kept the announcement tucked in with family photographs.

In 2011 I lost Harold to the cancer he battled so daringly all those years, long past any predictions. We had a memorial for him in his beloved redwood grove at our home in Healdsburg. While friends and family spoke about this wonderful man—my sweetheart, lover, and fellow walker through the world—Tandin lit one hundred eight yak-butter oil lamps in a small temple in Thimphu to ease Harold's passing into his next life. He wanted me to come and do the same.

Three years later I did.

I flew to a country still familiar, yet modernizing rapidly, with signs of construction everywhere. Tandin's aunt had just passed, and we spent days with monks, family, and friends, observing their traditions of mourning and remembrance. I sat for hours listening to mesmerizing chanting that brought Harold back for me more easily than I could have believed. Grandfather was older and more delicate, but very welcoming. When I asked if he would let me record his praying, he pulled me close, his voice rising and falling in a prayer he had probably performed millions of times. In many ways the trip was a homecoming, a return to something no longer odd and foreign.

One afternoon Tandin and I went to the small temple near the family home, where a monk took us into a special altar room filled with rows of yak-butter lamps, like Christian votive candles. They left me alone and, with soft chanting in the background, I lit one hundred eight lamps. At first, it seemed an enormous task. But as I neared the last lamp, I slowed down. It felt as if Harold were there with me. I wished, then, for one hundred eight more, or maybe to never stop.

During my visit, we spent much of the time in Thimphu; but Tandin and I also travelled to some of the areas we had trekked together. On our way to Bumthang, in the east, we had an unexpected meeting with his father in the mountains near his remote village. We shared yak-butter tea near the new packed-earth home he was building, and I was invited to pound dirt into one wall.

As we drove farther along those still-harrowing mountain roads, Tandin's phone rang. It was his mother, calling from Thimphu. He pulled over to the side of the road, spoke with her briefly, then beamed at me.

"I have never spoken to my mother and my father in the same day before! And you are here with me as well. It is a most auspicious day."

Late that night in Bumthang, the hotel we were staying in caught fire.

The fire was behind the stairs, my only exit path.

Once again it was Tandin and I, and few alternatives.

I trusted he would save me. Somehow his confidence became mine. He grabbed my arm, and we ran down the stairs.

As I stumbled out through the deserted lobby, Tandin ran back up the same threatened stairway—the older man staying down the hall from me was still in his room. As I stood outside, other people appeared, exiting the building wrapped in blankets, dazed and scared.

Tandin finally emerged, nearly carrying the confused gentleman. An ancient piece of firefighting equipment noisily bounced toward us along the pitted dirt road from Bumthang.

"I think we got everyone out," Tandin told me, as we stood and watched the firefighters battle the flames.

Fate or luck had kept Tandin awake that night, talking

to a fellow guide. Tandin smelled the smoke and was able to raise the alarm and save everyone staying in that hotel, including me.

His half-brother Tashi worked at a hotel nearby. We drove over and pounded on their door—seemingly forever, since it was the middle of the night. In spite of their initial shock, we were warmly welcomed inside.

As I get older I find fewer rational explanations for both the pain and the blessings fate showers upon me. The mathematical precision of the logic I studied in college has been tempered by life's impossible curves. I do, however, often return to Harold's conversation with Grandfather. I can see both of them, sitting in that intimate room, sussing each other out, deciding how much to trust. Deciding to believe in each other.

On this recent trip to Bhutan, as I walked into Tandin's marital home for the first time, I met his mother-in-law and was greeted joyously by his wife Chimmi, whom I knew from Bangkok. As we hugged, I saw two small people hiding in the doorway. The older and braver boy pulled his sister forward. They both stood before me—a complete stranger, someone from faraway. Sure that they would run to their mother, I stepped back so they wouldn't be frightened. Instead, big smiles broke out on little Palbar and Dechen's faces.

"Hi Granny!" they shouted, both running over to hug me.

I was no stranger.

3 TRIESTE: WHERE MEMORY STARTS

"No! I don't want to go! Don't make me leave!"
The child clings, sobbing, to a slender, silver-haired man. His gentle eyes tear up as he enfolds her in a warm embrace. Her curly blond hair covers both their faces.

It is a scene you could easily imagine if the child were being torn away from her home. But this girl is leaving a crowded barracks in a refugee camp. Tired of exile, after waiting four long, miserable years, this is her family's big day. The year is 1954, and they are confirmed on a ship to America.

I was that child, the one who couldn't bear to leave my beloved adopted grandfather or the only home I had ever known. I wanted to stay in Trieste, with my *Dyadya Zhenya*.

I didn't get my way.

We boarded a train and headed for Genoa—and our ship.

Late-afternoon sun glows on the smoothed stones of a

well-dressed cosmopolitan city. People relax in cafés and women's heels echo off cobblestones. Red liquid gleams in crystal goblets, as our table sways gently on a canal full of fishing boats. Our hotel is but a short stroll away, perched on the waterfront. A waitress delivers plates of small lobsters and smoked meats, smiling a *"Buon appetito."*

Trieste has adorned herself as if in welcome, seemingly bent on making it a challenge to remember our time of displacement.

"I bet you don't remember anything like this," my brother Sasha says.

"Hardly," I reply.

But what do I remember?

More than sixty years separates me from my arrival as an infant in this city in 1950. It was the final exile for us—a family forced to flee too many times. I am now determined to document that history in a book, so my brother and I are exploring our mother's homeland.

Before we head into the depths of Croatia and Serbia, we are spending a few days in Trieste, Italy, where our own childhoods began.

Our family had spent hundreds of years in the Balkans before having to flee. Trieste was just a short interval in that context. But for me, it represented my entire early childhood. I keep searching for a way to connect to it.

What is it about this city that defines me?

That first arrival as infants had not been in luxury. We didn't stay in a sophisticated hotel, nor did we savor delicacies or loll about in classy cafés. Stateless exiles, we spent four years waiting in an overcrowded refugee camp—*Campo San Sabba*. We shared that fate of disinheritance with this very city, for at that time it was a post-war no-man's-land. Trieste was being fought over by several countries. None, on the contrary, desired my family.

Sasha is my sole remaining link to this world. We have never been back together.

The morning after our arrival, Sasha and I set off for the nearby village of Opičina, which overlooks Trieste from rocky karst hills. Opičina was our point of arrival in an alien world, where a tented intake camp had been set up to accommodate those in a flight caused by the evolving Cold War. It was where the harsh reality of displacement—crowding and discomfort—sank in for my parents. The fact that they carried me with them, a crying infant, only made it all that much harder.

Now Sasha and I weave through an affluent Middle-European city that balances walking areas with cars and busses, eventually finding our way to a funicular that climbs a thousand feet in just minutes. That old blue tramcar—the twin of a favorite in San Francisco—feels almost familiar on this exploration, but it is the last remnant of an earlier era. It abandons us at its terminus.

Sasha and I wander aimlessly around Opičina, searching for a field, for old tents, for memories. Instead we find a pleasant but anonymous suburb that elicits no emotion and triggers no recognition.

We walk back toward the tram station, to a promontory overlooking Trieste and the winding Adriatic coast toward Slovenia and Croatia. It glows in the clearing light, welcoming the ships that dot the sea.

An old man on a walk pauses to point out a trail hugging a steep cliff.

"*Ecco la strada Napoleonica*," he says, explaining that Napoleon had planned a triumphant entry into Trieste—but was derailed by his exile in Elba. Sasha catches my eye. One more exile.

We follow the trail toward the next town, passing people picking wild asparagus. We watch rock climbers and dodge mountain bikers. We approach a coffee shop and consider stopping, but a Moroccan man out front won't stop trying to sell us brooms. He bewails the lack of jobs in Italy and asks us to adopt him and take him to America. He promises to quickly learn the language.

When we need directions, I ask a woman who turns out to have an instantly recognizable accent. We chat as we walk, she in Slovenian, Sasha and I in Serbian. Surprisingly, we understand each other easily. She tells us eighty percent of her town speaks Slovenian, and it is used in school and business. The border is not far, but they are native locals, not immigrants. It has always been their language. This Balkan interweaving is something we find everywhere as we explore the area.

Before Sasha and I leave Trieste for our mother's birthplace in Croatia, we explore what is left of Campo San Sabba. We have recently visited my Aunt Galya in the San Francisco flat where she fed me babka noodles as a child and chocolate cakes until she could no longer bake.

Galya's face lit up as she shared her memories. She made us find a photograph of her with my Uncle Shura, walking outside the rice factory—*risiera*—that was their housing at the camp. The picture showed two handsome young people grinning broadly—thin but neatly dressed. Only the brick wall behind them offered a clue to the environment.

"It was just a dark open space on the second floor of the abandoned factory," Galya said, remembering as if it were last month rather than sixty years ago. "There were no walls. We strung up old blankets to separate tiny spaces where we slept. There was a common table for eating."

"Sometimes in the evening we would move aside the blankets and open up the space. We would shove the beds away and somebody would bring out an accordion." Her face and voice became animated. "I remember one night in particular. I was having such a good time that I got up on the table and danced!" She laughed, vaguely remembering Shura getting angry with her.

When my American friends hear that as a child I lived for years in a refugee camp, sharing a small compartment in an abandoned army barracks with five people, they imagine only misery. I, however, remember being surrounded by love. My trauma lay in leaving for America and abandoning my beloved Dyadya Zhenya, my adopted grandfather. I knew no other world, and I reveled in mine. I didn't know other children didn't have brown stubs for teeth, or that walls were supposed to reach the floor and be thicker than cardboard. I didn't know what privacy was, nor that clothes could be bought in shops. I didn't know you could wander freely in towns, live in houses, or that other parents had jobs.

Galya's story of dancing on a table—shared shortly before she left us—confirmed that a zest for living has more to do with who you are than your circumstances. The Campo couldn't break our spirit. To the contrary, it birthed my unquenchable thirst to experience life.

When we lived in the Campo, around 1950, it was filled with White Russians—anti-communist forces that fought the Communist Bolsheviks in the Russian Civil War—like my father who had fled Russia many years earlier. Now, Stalin's expansion of communism throughout the Eastern Bloc had put their lives at risk. They were fleeing again, in the hopes that some country would offer them shelter.

Some years ago, when I took my mother to revisit Trieste, we learned that Campo San Sabba had a much uglier past. During World War II, it had been a concentration camp—the only one in Italy with crematoria. Not only the utter inhumanity of that evil, but its being followed by housing homeless refugees in that same space after the war ended, tore me apart. It's something I struggle with to this day. A few years later, I ran sobbing out of the movie *Life is Beautiful* when I recognized it was set in our Campo.

It took years for Italy to acknowledge that inhumane part of its history and declare the Campo a memorial, the *Risiera di San Sabba Monumento Nazionale*.

As we arrive at the Campo now, Sasha and I decide to find the precise spot where Galya's photograph was taken.

The area has been industrialized but shows signs of decay. We walk through characterless streets of run-down buildings and abandoned rail tracks. Finally we recognize the brick building that had been the old factory.

We approach what is now the memorial, comparing the site to Gayla's old photo, and step inside. The corner where our aunts and uncles lived is familiar, but their second-floor space is closed off.

Heading back outside, across the street from the Risiera, Sasha and I discover that the barracks where we lived were torn down. They have been replaced by a Coop grocery store warehouse.

As we continue exploring the area, eventually we find the spot where the photograph was taken, back near the Risiera. After, we wander around some more, circling the block and wandering uphill without feeling much connection.

Until I do.

Sixty years after we went to America, next to our old barracks area I find something I didn't know I had been seeking. I stand and point downhill at a crumbling retaining wall, a spot that instantly transports me to the past. I am three years old again.

As I stare at the rubble, Sasha gets a frown on his face that I remember from childhood. I am suddenly his baby sister again.

I can't resist. I climb over the broken wall and slide through shards of glass and old tin cans. It is the only unchanged spot along the street. Sasha laughs and follows.

It is the site of the first dream I remembered as a child—and I remember it still.

I don't know what other children dream about. Princes? Rainbows? Toys?

I dreamt of an old suitcase.

The dream was so vivid, I awoke thinking it had been real. Now I relive the scene that followed when I woke the next morning.

"But Mama," I shouted, "I know it's there! I saw it! We have to go look."

I pulled Mama's hand. I knew there was an old suitcase abandoned in a dirty field, and it was full of clothes. We needed those clothes, and I wanted her to share in my special find. They would all be so excited. I led her through the rubble and broken glass, rusty barbed wire, broken bricks. The suitcase had to be there.

It is the one spot in all of Trieste that resonates deeply with me. It was the setting for the dream of a child for whom old clothes in a battered suitcase were such a treasure that she made her mother crawl through that dirt field. It was years before I accepted what the adults kept telling me—that it had been "just a dream."

There was no treasure chest in Trieste. Not then. Not now.

We leave the area and head back toward town.

Over the following days we learn that Trieste experienced a major financial collapse when the Berlin Wall fell. Trieste's harbor, in particular, shows the effects of the crisis. It seems a new wave of refugees has found their way here.

We wander through the abandoned Port of Trieste, around hauntingly beautiful remnants of a long gallery built of giant stones. We find makeshift homeless shelters built into the colonnades and dark-skinned men playing cricket. They tell me they are from Afghanistan; hundreds of them—refugees from the war—with nothing to do. They are gracious to us—the only light-skinned people in this bizarre enclave. I want to tell them that I, too, was once homeless in this town, but we don't have a common language.

Sasha and I continue our walk along the waterfront and emerge onto a beautiful esplanade laid with half-moon-patterned bricks that were set by hand and require constant maintenance. I try to take a photo of a man relaying bricks, but he quickly steps out of the scene. When he speaks to a friend, I catch an accent and ask where he is from.

"Belgrade," he replies, reluctantly.

"I was born there!" I exclaim in Serbian.

He tells me his neighborhood, smiling broadly upon learning I am now from America. When he nonetheless still won't let us take his picture, we realize he is probably not legal here.

Later, a young pregnant couple strolling around the harbor asks to have their picture taken.

"Kosovo," the father-to-be says, in reply to my usual question.

"*Govorite po Srpski?* Do you speak Serbian?" I ask.

"No!" He is emphatic. "Albanian!"

He takes his camera back and walks off. I am no longer an American—or even someone who can be trusted. I am the enemy who destroyed his country.

In the late-afternoon light we head back to our canal-side café, to an aperitif and some pampering. It is an environment I am comfortable with, a way of traveling and living that is familiar. Having started out with so little, at this stage of my life affluence and ease is something I have gotten used to.

Soon Sasha and I will explore Balkan countries torn apart in the wars that broke up Yugoslavia in the 1990s. Our relatives are scattered over what was once a single country but is now divided into multiple states. We can barely guess what conditions we will find there. Trieste has started to offer some clues.

There is no escaping the refugees—from neighboring as well as distant lands. In her final book, *Trieste and the Meaning of Nowhere*, Jan Morris, one of the great travel writers of our times, defines the city as "an allegory of limbo."

For my parents limbo is exactly what it was. Torn from a successful life in Belgrade, they spent four years of uncertainty and discomfort.

In limbo.

Trieste was first part of ancient Illyria, then of the Roman Empire. It was part of the Austrian and Hungarian empires—with a brief invasion by Napoleon—until World War I ended that era. In 1921 the northern coast of the Adriatic was granted to Italy. Once again, after the Second World War—when my family lived there—Trieste went up for grabs, fought over by Italy and Yugoslavia.

It was eventually granted to Italy. Jutting like a pinky finger into Slavic territory, it looks in many ways like a no-man's-land. Sasha and I now experience a city that is part of Italy, yet clearly also a part of the Balkans. A city buffeted by the Bura winds from the Adriatic as much as the shifting tides of one government after another. A city still as much Austro-Hungary and Slovenia as Italy. A city still a haven for lost souls.

Over my drink I ponder the role Trieste has played in my life. I say to Sasha, "I keep thinking of that walk around San Sabba. For me, that old camp really is where memory starts."

"Well yeah, we don't remember anything about Yugoslavia. Trieste and Opičina are where it all began for us."

"But I still can't figure out what role this town itself played in making me who I am—and why I'm so attached to it."

"Perhaps its continuous tie with displaced peoples explains your own perpetual wanderings," Sasha offers, taking another drink.

Over the next weeks, Sasha and I explore our family's past. From our mother's homeland in Istria to the Montenegro our ancestors fled in the seventeenth century when the Turks attacked. From the town in Bosnia where our father laid railroad tracks to the village of Petrovaradin in Serbia, where our mother shared her childhood with six sisters. In Medulin we discover an ongoing feud over the house of my mother's birth. In Novi Sad, over one hundred cousins come when we throw a lunch.

We go to Belgrade to see the hospital where I was born, the apartment we shared with my grandmother, and my grandfather's grave.

We connect to our past with an expanding sense of wonder and joy. But this is my family's past, not one I myself have lived.

My past started in Trieste.

Returning from San Sabba, Sasha and I walk back to our hotel, a distance of some ten miles. At one point we reach a cliff, unsure how to proceed. It makes me think about the two of us, at the edge of a cliff—a chasm, really. On one side, two little kids on their way to America—in clothes made by their mother from hand-me-downs—waving wildly as their train leaves the now-abandoned old Trieste station. On the other, two Americans in casual dress, staying at the finest hotel in town.

I came to an age of awareness in a land that belonged to no state, an equally stateless child. But that child felt loved in that land, and the memory of the love I felt there is deeply a part of me.

I had hoped to find remnants of the Trieste I left behind; instead I discover I have never really left.

4 BENEATH THE SURFACE

"*Proklete meduse!* Cursed jellyfish!"

The shout, accompanied by a fist aimed at God, startled me out of my reverie, as the sunset's glow lit the port town of Rovinj, across the Adriatic Sea from Venice.

The handsome fisherman and I both observed the same scene, his rage matching my joy. The water was filled with translucent flexible Frisbees, their center disks the dusty rose of my favorite childhood sweater. As I watched, transfixed, the creatures floated among the ropes of hundreds of boats. Children ran around in excitement, clapping hands and laughing at this mass invasion.

It was the spring of 2014. My brother Sasha and I were spending a month roaming around the beautiful peninsula of Istria, in Croatia, where our mother was born.

"*Uvek su tu?* Are they always here?" I asked, referring to the medusas.

Sasha and I were born in Belgrade, when the country was still called Yugoslavia. Our family was forced into political exile when we were babies, but our parents' commitment to their native tongues meant we grew up fluent in both our father's Russian and our mother's Croatian.

"They weren't here fifteen minutes ago. I haven't seen them often—they usually head elsewhere," the fisherman said, nodding toward Italy.

"They're beautiful!" I said, pointing my camera. "Like a modern-art painting."

By now the port was full of these creatures. People were gesticulating and talking about them. A young teen was trying to poke one of them with her foot.

"It's this strange wind from Africa that brought them here," a local woman said of the rapid, silent attack.

I nodded, knowing that the prevalent Bora winds start from the northeast and normally blow southwest, pushing debris away from the Dalmatian coast.

Milan, the fisherman, reluctantly acknowledged that the medusas were quite pretty. But he fervently hoped they would leave as quickly as they had arrived.

"They mess up the fishing lines, bite tourists' feet, and ruin the beaches!"

My joy at the first twenty turned to astonishment at what soon numbered in the thousands, dancing among reflections and shifting sparkles as a giant crimson sun sank slowly into the sea. Light shimmered around the edges of backlit clouds, and the church tower atop the old-town promontory was outlined in gold. I couldn't resist photographing the setting sun and gasped as a seagull floated into perfect position in the frame. Like the invisible tentacles of a medusa enveloping its unsuspecting prey, so Istria wrapped its arms around me, luring me into a dance of seduction to which I eagerly succumbed.

NEVER A STRANGER

Rovinj rises from the sea just a hundred kilometers south of Trieste, Italy. Its buildings amazingly unharmed in the various wars of the last century, it also boasts beautiful remains of ancient Roman fortifications. Cafés and shops dot narrow streets laid with pale-gold stones that glow when the sun is low, polished by centuries of footsteps.

Two evenings after the medusa invasion, Sasha and I were back at the water.

"The water is clear again," he commented. The jellyfish were gone.

Before I could respond, a tall, handsome local up ahead swore, "*Prokleto cvetanje!* Cursed flowering!"

We approached. Swirls of orange the color of both the sunset and his outfit sullied the water surrounding the local's boat.

"It wasn't there an hour ago!" he lamented.

The orange was an invasive algae bloom, also known as a "red tide." The man, who was dressed as Captain Nemo of the submarine Nautilus, feared the impact it would have on his glass-bottom boat business.

Sasha and I were mystified. The bloom was spreading through the water in random patterns.

"I've rarely seen this—and never before in the spring, only in midsummer."

The one bright spot in Croatia's economy was tourism. Captain Nemo feared the red tide could kill the Adriatic tourist season.

A day later we saw Captain Nemo laughing with his buddies. The red tide, like the medusas, was gone.

Friends at home in San Francisco raved about Croatia as a tourist destination. For me, Croatia was the place of disasters that started long before I was born, swept me and my family up, and caused our expulsion—which had continued until just a few years earlier. Could the tide have turned? I wanted to know. I wanted to go beneath the surface to learn what was happening in the countries of the former Yugoslavia, with which my family had such deep roots.

From Rovinj, Sasha and I wandered into the heart of Istria. We visited towns carved into mountaintops, some with stone walls that protected them from medieval marauders. Reminiscent of Tuscany maybe forty years ago, the interior countryside here was full of semi-abandoned and unexplored villages, hidden gems not yet discovered by the tourists pouring into the coastal towns and beaches.

In one such village, Tignane, we paused to look at a thick round table surrounded by twelve mushroom-shaped seats, all carved from giant slabs of local stone. Set under a huge, gnarled tree, it reminded me of a scene from *The Adventures of Asterix*.

Almost immediately, Sasha and I were approached by Attilio, a local who was turning eighty that week. He explained that the fifteenth century stone table was used when a chieftain died. The twelve eldest men in the village sat on the stone seats and spread their long beards into the center. A flea was dropped in the middle and watched carefully. The man whose beard it jumped onto first became the next leader.

While Attilio shared the story, another local appeared. Dorian's house abutted the open grassy area where the table was located. He had noticed our impromptu gathering and couldn't resist coming over to be a part.

"An early form of democracy," he said in jest, referring to the flea ritual. "Not any worse than our current one, as far as I can tell."

Dorian invited us over to his house, where he offered us a delicious homemade honey-flavored version of grappa called *medica*, after *med*, or honey. As he showed us his lovingly restored home, he also told us more about Tignane—and its woes.

Many of the village's buildings were abandoned, their beautiful ancient stonework crumbling. A complex bureaucracy kept ownership uncertain. Some buildings had apparently been left to descendants of families who had moved to Canada or South America or Australia.

Attilio explained that he and Dorian were among the few people still living in this town. He succinctly summarized why.

"There is no work, no jobs. The young people have all left."

On the way back to the coast, Sasha and I stopped at a restaurant in the ancient manor house of an old vineyard. The gnarled vines looked like desiccated gnomes. They reminded me of the Sonoma County I had moved to in the 1980s, before most of the old free-standing vines had succumbed to disease and been replaced by efficiently latticed rows.

After devouring some spit-roasted baby lamb, we met the vineyard owner, Zora, who joined us for a glass of their white wine and a chat.

"We noticed there is a lot of barren land. Will you be planting more vineyards and olive groves?" I asked.

Sonoma county had increased its vine-cultivated land a hundred-fold since I moved there, in response to market demand for its wines. My town of Healdsburg sometimes felt like one big wine-tasting room. So, Sasha and I knew what it was like to live in wine and olive country. Why was Istria so slow to capitalize on this bounty, now that communism and the wars were a thing of the past? Surely the free market would kick in here, as it had in Sonoma.

"We can't," Zora said, taking a sip of wine.

"What do you mean?" I wondered.

"You know Croatia has become a full member of the European Union."

"Yes. So, I imagine that will mean more investment opportunities," Sasha said. He assumed we would now be talking about the sort of over-development concerns we might discuss at home.

"Well, the European Union has very tight controls on agriculture."

"What does that mean?" I asked.

"It means we are not allowed to increase the number of grape vines or olive trees without approval. And since the market right now is weak, no approvals are being given."

Sasha and I just looked at her, astonished. We had been driving around the country naively inventing creative market opportunities to pull Croatia out of its economic misfortune. We had never imagined that their options—their very future—was tied to wine makers in Portugal or olive growers in Greece.

The next morning I wandered off on my own, ending up in a seaside village not far from Rovinj. It wasn't long before I made a new friend.

A well-toned middle-aged guy with dark wavy hair, he was winding his fishing nets. I seized the opportunity to snap some pictures.

"I'm Tania," I said, once I was satisfied I'd gotten some good shots.

"*Drago*," he replied. "Pleasure."

"*I meni je drago*," I said, "Pleased to meet you, too."

He smiled and kept working.

"I'm Tania," I reiterated, waiting for him to introduce himself. "And you are?"

"Drago," he repeated.

"Yes, pleased to meet you, too," I said again. "And your name is…"

"Drago."

I shot him another look of confusion. A split-second later, it hit me.

"Ah!" I exclaimed.

"I am pleased to me you," he laughed, "and it's my name!"

We wandered back to his fishing shack for an early glass of wine. I learned he had sold his home on the water, because prices exploded, and built a new one up on the hill, where tourists rarely ventured. He also told me there were only four fishermen left in the town and that the fish were mostly gone. He set his nets in the evening and gathered them in the morning, almost from habit rather than for the meager results.

"A few years ago the Europeans protected the tuna. Now the tuna eat all the smaller fish. We have almost nothing to catch."

I thought he, too, like the vineyard owner, might talk about the challenges of European Union membership. I was wrong. Instead, he told me that the industry on the coast was dying.

"There used to be a tuna processing plant over there," he said, pointing vaguely. "And lots of shipping in Rijeka. But we gave it all up to corruption."

"Did foreigners come in?"

"We didn't need foreigners! We did it to ourselves. We have an expression: *'Dva Hrvata, tri ladra,'*" he joked. It meant "two Croatians, three crooks," using the Italian word for "crook."

It was becoming more and more clear that the notion that government action could help rather than hinder seemed inconceivable to Croatians.

Drago and I chatted a bit more. He asked if I wanted to meet again that afternoon. It was tempting. The way he looked deep into my eyes. His smile. He certainly knew how to flirt. But Sasha and I were moving on. I would have to pass.

NEVER A STRANGER

Sasha and I had only planned to spend a few days in Rovinj. But the draw of the harbor in the evening light proved irresistible. We kept postponing our departure. Before we knew it, two weeks flew by as we continued exploring coastal and inland towns, making it back each night in time for our harborside aperitif.

One evening we were wandering around town enjoying the sunset, the scene like an impressionist painting: a waterside café, the air warm enough for patrons to sit outside; old stones glowing red; clouds positioning themselves as if posing for the best picture; church bells ringing; voices in Italian and Croatian.

We were in paradise.

As we strolled, we came upon a restaurant with a single rare lobster on offer. It was $150 a kilo. Local fish—including the fat-faced red groupers staring at us with bulging eyes—were around $50 a kilo.

Sasha and I struck up a conversation with a Macedonian waiter who worked at the restaurant. When we told him and his buddies that lobster in the U.S. was plentiful again due to tightly controlled catches over the past few years, they looked at us with disbelief. *It ain't gonna happen here*, I read in his raised eyebrows.

Hard to believe that when my late husband and I had brought my mother to Istria in 1992, we ate huge platters of some of the best shellfish I've ever had—for just a few dollars.

Since arriving in Croatia, I had been looking for a book published in Yugoslavia in the 1980s called *The Scent of Rain*

in the Balkans. I had the English version, but I wanted to read it in its native language while traveling in the country.

The next day I found a small bookshop and asked if they had the book.

"I am sorry, that book was published in Serbia. I cannot sell it to you here," said an attractive young saleswoman.

It was the fourth bookstore where I had asked about the book; yet she was the first person to tell me why I couldn't find it anywhere. This was Croatia. They wouldn't carry a book published in Serbia. It hit me hard.

Even after I left the store, the strain in the saleswoman's voice as she told me the truth stayed with me. I wanted to learn more about the Serbian-Croatian-Bosnian tension remaining from the wars.

Shortly after, I got the chance.

Sasha and I were staying in a vacation rental owned by a Bosnian-Serb couple, Ivan and Maria. Leaving Bosnia when they were young, they spent forty years working in Austria while building their house in Istria. Their daughters had married Austrians, but they all held Croatian passports, *"just in case."*

During the war of the 1990s, Muslim neighbors whom they had known and been friendly with for years murdered their Christian parents in Bosnia. Long after the war ended, Ivan and Maria finally went back and, after an exhaustive search, found their parents' bodies buried in a field near their old house.

I heard a number of such stories—of atrocities, of reprisals, of simple disagreements between neighbors. They never got easier to accept. I had wonderful interactions with most of the people I met in Istria. Would that have been the case if our family had stayed? Or would I, too, have been pushed to take sides? Would I share the rage or envy or guilt experienced by so many here who had lived through the wars?

Ivan and Maria had no interest in going back to Bosnia, but they didn't feel at home in Austria, either. They liked Istria well enough but found the locals hard to deal with and couldn't fit in completely.

"They all think," said Maria, "that we went abroad and got wealthy while they stayed home and suffered. Well, we worked hard for what we have. While they led normal lives, we worked at full-time jobs in Austria during the week, then drove here every weekend and slaved to build this house. Who are they to think we had it easy?"

A few days earlier, Sasha and I had encountered a nimble older woman picking wild asparagus in the forest.

"Most people stay on the beach or in the cafés," she said, surprised to run into us.

She looked down at the large bundle in her arms and laughed. "My son and his wife are visiting from America, and I am trying to convince them to stay here."

The wild asparagus stalks were as thin as knitting needles. I had bought bundles of them from people standing along roadsides, taking them home to fry into eggs and pasta. The wild asparagus was slightly bitter to the taste, relating to our farmed varieties perhaps as arugula does to butter lettuce. Unlike the mushrooms I spend so many hours seeking in my forested hills at home, I had yet to learn the wild asparagus's secret hiding places. The woman knew exactly where to look.

"Is the asparagus a bribe?" I asked. "It would work for

me."

"I would clear the forest of all its asparagus if such a bribe worked!" she exclaimed, laughing at herself and handing me a stalk to try. But there was no convincing her American daughter-in-law to move to this remote backwater.

"She thinks we are all barbarians, killing each other. I know she believes that the nearest good supermarket is in Germany and that our language sounds like we are arguing no matter what we say."

"Well . . ." I was a bit taken aback.

"Yes," she continued, before I could reply. Her eyes were close to tears. "I, too, can understand how she might think that. The world's newspapers were full of—"

"The asparagus is amazing," I interjected, trying to change the subject.

Following my lead, she proceeded to tell me spring had come early that year.

"I was picking asparagus in month two, rather than three," she explained, handing me a few more stalks. She then headed off in search of a product precious enough to convince a skeptical daughter-in-law to see the paradise through the gloom.

"Month two," "month three"—I thought the designation strange. I even heard a young man who had been working as an *au pair* in London say he had returned in "month seven" the previous year.

"Why do you refer to it as month seven?" I asked. "I've heard that form a lot here."

He grinned and rolled his eyes. "You know, it's so absurd. We used to call the months *Juli*, *Avgust*, and so on. Everyone understood. Then we had to separate ourselves from the Serbs. And those months became *Srpanj* and *Kolovoz*. How odd is that? It's the *vlasti*," he said.

Vlasti is the generic word I heard so often in the area, meaning the powers that control the residents.

"They needed to make us feel different, to remind us that once we were victims, but now we are victors. What can you do?"

The new words derive from archaic Slavic terms. Before the war, Serbian and Croatian were almost the same language—even called Serbo-Croatian—with the primary difference being pronunciation. The young man wasn't the only local I spoke with who found the new words annoying.

Near the end of our stay in Rovinj, Sasha and I met up with my friend Nikola and his wife Ana at a beautiful café in Rovinj. They had driven from Zagreb to visit us.

Nikola sat downwind, so the smoke from his endless cigarettes wouldn't blow in our faces. He had quit some years before, just prior coming to California to climb Mount Whitney with us. But he started again under the stress of life back in Croatia.

After the birth of his children, Nikola had gone back to his job as a computer consultant. Scuba instruction, which he enjoyed briefly as a single man, was fun but didn't support a family. His wife was a marketing executive with a start-up, working part-time so she could spend more time with the boys. On the surface, their lives seemed familiar and comfortable.

When I asked his thoughts about the ongoing effects of the wars, he replied quickly.

"We don't have time to think about the Serbs!" He shook his head and ground the cigarette out on his saucer. "Things are so bad, we can only think about the state of our own economy. The right-wing nationalist governments of the last fifteen years have brought us to our knees. They have destroyed our country."

"Don't you see any signs of improvement?" Sasha asked. Nikola's comments felt so incongruous with the bustling café; the gorgeous portside setting; the restaurants; our impressions before coming.

"Yes, we have finally elected a more liberal government. At least it's not all about hatred, but it may be too late for us," he replied.

"You know, we came out of this war thinking we were heroes, giants, better than the others," he said, becoming reflective. "We need a sense of reality."

He thought his sons would probably leave the country as soon as they were old enough. As citizens of the European Union, he believed they could eventually find work abroad.

"There are no jobs, little industry, few prospects, and little discussion about a positive future."

"But Nikola, isn't tourism booming here?" I persisted. "Many of my friends are visiting. I thought things were improving."

"American tourists mostly come on cruise ships," he said.

I nodded. I was well aware of that. I was not, however, aware of what he explained next.

"Americans don't fly into Croatia and stay in a hotel. They pull into port on their luxury ships—mostly in Dubrovnik and towns here in Istria, maybe the islands—and everyone disembarks for a few hours. They wander around, sometimes have coffee, and maybe buy a trinket. Mostly they take pictures with their phones."

Nikola looked around as if trying to see through our eyes the country he loved but was so worried about. He lit a new cigarette, took a puff, and continued.

"Then those people get back on the boat to have dinner, party, and sleep. They leave almost no money in the local economy. The tourists who spend money here are mostly Germans, and they," he said, chuckling, "are far more prudent than you Americans in their spending."

His comments resonated. From the outside, towns like Poreč and Rovinj looked vibrant and alive. People were friendly and warm. Yet we had heard so many locals express a deep concern about their future. The recession of 2007 had hit just as they were putting their feet back on the ground after the wars. And although Croatia was now a member of the European Union, nearly twenty percent of the population was unemployed. They were seeing only minor improvements, however rosy it might look from the outside to visitors.

I had naively hoped the tide had started to turn. The civil war was a thing of the past. European Union membership had been attained. The Dalmatian coast was becoming a highly desirable tourist destination.

But, in our conversations with the locals, Sasha and I were constantly reminded that the view from the outside—like an envelope hiding its contents—couldn't convey what was really going on inside. The reality was complicated and difficult to make sense of. It was as hard to predict the long-term outcome for Croatia as for the European Union as a whole.

Glowing from a brisk walk by the sea, Ana put an abrupt end to our conversation. The four of us headed to a favorite restaurant, where the host greeted us like family and poured sparkling wine in welcome. Leaving our earlier concerns behind, we behaved like the carefree American tourists the local economy so badly needed. We indulged in the hedonistic pleasures offered by the surroundings—truffles, wild asparagus, and lobsters, accompanied by a crisp white wine. We then took a stroll in the storybook setting, talking lightheartedly until, much to everyone's chagrin, Nikola and Ana had to leave for Zagreb.

"You know," Sasha said, as parting hugs were exchanged, "we've fallen in love with this place. You'll be seeing a lot more of us."

Croatia's challenges did nothing to detract from its incomparable beauty or appeal. There was no question we would be back.

Nikola beamed, then grinned as if his own thoughts surprised him. He looked around at the crystal-clean water, the glowing stones, and the bustling town. And then, exhaling deeply, he seemed to let go of something tight in his chest.

5 HOMELAND

I wondered yet again: had I really agreed to fly on a one-way ticket into a remote backwater of 1977 Communist Russia, a country repressed by fear and impoverished by incompetent bureaucracy, one my father fled as an infant and couldn't believe his daughter was braving?

My family, Don Cossacks, had lived for centuries on the Don River between Moscow and Stalingrad. The Cossacks, although mostly peasants, were staunch supporters of the tsar and represented the last stand of resistance to the Communist Revolution, losing the final battle in 1920.

When I was a child, my grandmother told me stories of that final battle. How the family, following the White Army, repeatedly left their village and returned. How, by the last retreat, there was no time to dig up the silver she had buried under the back doorstep to their house, abandoned to the dust of history. My grandmother was long gone, but in my mind that silver in its dirt grave halfway around the world lived on, my sole keepsake beyond the small gold stars she had always worn dangling from her ears. I wanted to see where our story began. I wanted to retrieve what my grandmother was forced to leave behind. I wanted to dig up that dirt.

I would be heading north from Stalingrad to Uryupinsk, in a ten-passenger WWII biplane converted for commercial use. In front of me a man stared intently into the open cockpit, leaning in as if he would steer from his seat if he could. I had seen him and the two pilots drink a quick shot of vodka in the cafeteria before departure.

"What are you doing?" I asked.

"I am the observer," the man replied proudly.

The Communist party had observers everywhere. They had broken my camera, pawed through my luggage, read my notes. Now this guy was making sure of what—that the pilots didn't hijack us?

The plane rattled into action and sped down the runway. The noise was deafening. The plane shivered and groaned. Only three hundred miles, it took an interminable three hours, during which the shaking didn't abate. A confident flier who rarely feels queasy, almost instantly I started retching and then vomiting, my head in a bag for the entire trip. Perhaps I should have joined the men for that early-morning vodka shot.

When we finally landed, I couldn't get up. I couldn't think. I could barely breathe. Everyone else deplaned. Finally, holding onto the bag—embarrassed to leave it behind—I crawled to the door.

We were in an abandoned field, dead grass all around. At the bottom of the stairs, a man with a paunch and an official-looking chauffeur's hat waited.

"*Ah, vi Amerikanka!*" he said. You're the American.

"*Kak vi znali?*" I replied. How did you know?

"There was no one else left."

He introduced himself as Yura, the chauffeur for the president of the flaxseed-oil factory, and the proud driver of the only private car in the district. He explained that his boss had loaned him to me for my stay. Did I want to go to my hotel or straight toward the village of Kulikov?

"I have a hotel?" The town had no cars. The airport was a dirty field. My expectations were low.

"Yes," he explained, proudly. "Our town has a hotel because we have a sister city in Czechoslovakia and our visitors need a place to stay."

I decided to head to the hotel. I desperately needed to wash up.

No American had ever visited the modest but clean hotel, far beyond any approved tourist areas. The price for the night was one ruble, less than two dollars at the official exchange rate.

The forms were in Russian. I transliterated my town of Minneapolis into Cyrillic: Минияполис. There was no line for state or country.

The receptionist peered at the form carefully, then said, "That's in the north, right?"

I was impressed with her knowledge of U.S. geography. "Why, yes. How did you know?"

"I could tell by your accent," she replied. "It is vaguely Siberian."

My father had left Russia as an infant, and I had never set foot here before. All the same, my knowledge of the language was good enough that this woman, who had never been anywhere else, took me for a native. It was an amazing testament to the uniquely powerful Russian concept of *ródina*, or homeland.

The showers in the hotel were off for the day, and there was no hot water. I washed up in the sink.

Before setting off, I asked Yura if we could buy some water. We stopped in five stores, all empty and deserted. What did these people eat? Finally he took me back to the hotel, where they gave me a large bottle of apple juice and a chipped glass.

I had been unable to find a map that included the remote village of Kulikov, where my father was born. However, I was fluent in the language, stubborn and determined.

My father's brother Shura was eight when they left, the oldest son and now patriarch of the scattered family. He had sketched a map of the village and proudly pointed out their family home, telling me it was "the only two-story house in the village."

My grandfather, whom I had never met, was a *kulak*, a peasant who took advantage of land reforms passed in 1906 to develop a wheat-trading business and rise above his class. Uncle Shura drew the *ambar*, or granary, on the map. It was across from his aunt's house, near the creek and the church, and around the corner from the train station. This final detail—that the village was important enough to have a train stop—was the clue that still had me on the hunt.

Yura knew the train station. "The Jarizhenskaya station," he said, "is near your village of Kulikov. Do you know any other details?"

I did. The previous evening in Stalingrad I had repeated an act I had performed in countless cities around the world: I had scoured the phone book for an Amochaev. I had never found anyone beyond my immediate family; but Stalingrad had two, and I had met one of them: Oleg. While neither of us knew enough about our families to figure out if we were related, his mother lived in our village of Kulikov. I had agreed to look her up and tell her that he was well and would write soon.

"We are looking for Maria Afanasievna Amochaeva at number 6, Gorkii Street," I told Yura.

We quickly reached the outskirts of the city and bounced onto a dirt road.

"This," he said, "will soon be the highway to Moscow!"

"Soon" was a relative term. Weeds abounded. No equipment was in sight. I couldn't help but wonder how soon.

"And what do you think of this car?" Yura asked.

It was a comfortable Volga limousine. I told him how fortunate I felt that his boss let me have use of it.

"Do you own a car?"

"I do."

"Is it like this?"

"Oh, no," I said. "It is much smaller."

"Of course," he nodded, likely visualizing the tin cans of Eastern Europe rather than my late-model sports car. "Did you wait a long time for it?"

"No, we don't actually have to wait for cars."

He mulled this over for a while.

"But you do have shortages, don't you?" He was searching for common ground.

I wracked my brain and remembered a true story.

"Last year," I said, "there was a run on toilet paper. It was started by a rumor that the toilet-paper company was going out of business." I didn't mention that it was a comedy-show gag gone awry.

"Yes, that happens a lot here. But could you buy a truck? Or a bus?"

"If I could afford it, I could."

"Surely that can't be. *Ne mozhet bits*. How would you do that?"

I had never actually thought about it. "I'm really not sure," I said. "I guess I would go to a company that sells them."

"Would you need permission from the powers, *ot*

vlasti?"

"Well,"—now it was I who stretched to find common ground—"I would have to get a special driver's license to operate a large vehicle."

"Ah. They would probably use that to prevent you from buying one," Yura said knowingly, in collusion with me against the bureaucracy.

I found myself torn, as so often happened on this trip, between wanting to share a bit of my life and not wanting to point out just how desperate theirs seemed to me. It was a fine line to walk. The previous evening Oleg had proudly showed me the latest miracle installed in his family's apartment, to the envy of the neighbors: a sink where cold and hot water merged into one faucet rather than coming out separately. I did my best to act impressed.

As I was leaving, Oleg opened the top of his greatest treasure: a small piano bought with his black-market earnings as a dentist nights and weekends. He withdrew a clear plastic sleeve with four colored felt pens and offered it with both hands, saying: "This is for you, to take back and remember us by."

"That's ... those are the ones Cousin Igor brought back from Germany," his wife stuttered, the pain of loss clear in her voice.

He insisted. I didn't have the heart to tell Oleg that at home I had a drawer full of felt pens.

Back in the limousine, my conversation with Yura was interrupted by the appearance of the train station. An elderly man walked along the tracks. We pulled over to ask about our destination.

"Can you tell me, *tovarisch*, how to find 6 Gorkii Street?" Yura asked the man.

"Where do you think you are, Moscow?" came the gruff reply. "We are in the boonies, *mi v derevnye*, not the big city.

Who are you looking for?"

"We are looking for Maria Afanasievna Amochaeva," I interjected.

"Ah. Why didn't you say so? She is in her front yard with Efim Ivanovich, as always. Take the first right, it's a hundred *arshins* up the road." I thought arshins had died with the Old Testament, but the driver knew it was a measure just short of a yard. We easily found the two friends sipping tea at a table in front of a small house.

Convincing them of my identity was much more problematic.

"What do you mean, you're from America but your father was born here?" said the frowning woman, her gray hair circling her head in a neatly tucked braid. "That's not possible, there's no one in America from here!"

She was almost right. The escape had been a close call. My grandfather had loaded the family, including four children and his mother, onto his horse cart and fled across hundreds of miles of war-torn country to the town of Yvpatoria on the Black Sea. In late 1920, carrying a large bag of wheat and a single suitcase, they boarded one of the last ships taking refugees out of the country. They survived by mixing the wheat with saltwater and baking it on the ship's steam-pipe exhaust vent. The ship tried to dock in Istanbul but was refused entry. Gallipoli was taking only military refugees, no children.

Finally, they landed on the Greek island of Limnos. Many of the refugees on Limnos died of starvation and disease, but the wheat fed my family until they were given asylum by the King of Serbia, where I was born.

I started explaining: "Well, his father took his family away during the revolution..."

"Likely story." The old woman spat at the ground.

"Why would I lie to you?"

"Why wouldn't you? And who's he, with the fancy car, driving you around like some kind of princess? What are you doing here? We don't know anything. We have nothing to say."

There was something about her steely strength that reminded me of my grandmother. She clearly assumed I had been sent for some nefarious reason. Was this as far as I would get?

"Marusia, Marusia, wait a minute. Let the young lady tell us what she wants. Maybe she can explain," counseled the man, Efim. Tall and thin and around the same age, which I seriously overestimated as around eighty, he quickly became my ally, loosening up as my chauffeur wisely withdrew.

"Well, all I know is that my grandfather's name was Ivan Minaevich Amochaev," I explained, "and that he had a house and an ambar here. When the Red Army defeated the Whites for the last time, they escaped to the Black Sea. Almost forty years later they ended up in America. My uncle was eight when they left, and he drew me a map." I turned to Efim. "Why doesn't she believe me?"

Efim swept his upturned palm across the emptiness that surrounded us. "Well, you see, *dorogaia*, dear, no one survived."

"What do you mean?"

"When the Reds came in, they lined up and shot all the men and boys over twelve years old. No one got away. You're the first person in nearly sixty years who ever arrived claiming to be from here."

His words suddenly explained the silence of decades, all the letters gone unanswered. I had trouble grasping the scope of the tragedy, before he continued.

"But you have nothing to gain that I can imagine, so I am prepared to believe you. Do you have that map?"

"Oh my God! Were you here?" I wanted him to keep talking. I needed to learn more.

"We were infants," he said, "but we grew up with stories of the horror. Marusia lost her father, her brothers. She can't bear to think about it all."

I pulled out my map, and we huddled over it.

"Theirs was the two-story house, right here. I was told it had become a tea house, a *chaiovnia*, after the revolution."

"*Milaya*," Efim said, dear one, "there has never been a two-story house in this village, but let me see this. There was a tea shop at that corner. Let's walk over there."

We wandered around with the map. The town hadn't grown since my family left, and the remaining skeleton matched the sketch. I realized that my uncle's little-boy mind had kept a larger-than-life image of his father's home. All the same, we soon found not only the house but even the ambar.

The neighboring village became the collective farm, and the young people had been moved there, Efim explained. Most of the homes in Kulikov were abandoned, the church was torn down, and there was no need for a school anymore.

"We're just left with dust and memories," he reflected. "And we don't let the memories go back too far."

Stalin's collectivization campaign, which destroyed the final private ownership of land by peasants and wiped out all kulaks as enemies of the people, became real for me in a way it never had in my history classes at Russian school in San Francisco.

I approached the house, the forlorn and crumbling single-story, brown *isba* that would eventually disappoint Uncle Shura. I circled the faded wood fence that surrounded it, checked the gate. It was all shut tight. I walked around and shot a few pictures, trying to imagine who I might have been, who my father might have been. The gap was too wide; we simply wouldn't have existed.

"Who owns this now?" I asked.

"No one owns anything, here, *zolotko*," golden one, Efim said, inadvertently using my father's childhood nickname for me. "No one has lived here in a long time. Everything belongs to the state. We aren't allowed to go inside or touch anything."

I could tell this gentle man would be uncomfortable if I opened the gate and walked up to embrace the house, as I longed to do. People had been beaten into submission by a system that spread fear and terror as a way of life. In an abandoned backwater miles from anywhere, that authority still controlled their actions, from their fear of strangers to blind obedience to power.

My father, forced to flee a Communist dictatorship yet

again as an adult, had carried some of those scars. I, on the contrary, had grown up in a country that took my family in with little more than the clothes on our backs and allowed me to become a woman unafraid of challenges, knowing how to aim high and break barriers.

I was at the heart of so many memories: my grandmother's, my uncle's, mine. The rough wooden fence with its missing slats, leaning precariously, was no barrier to me. It would be so easy to open that gate, or climb over it. To dig a hole at the back-door stoop. To search for my treasure, my grandmother's silver. I had no idea what it really was, just that it was something I had wanted my whole life. But taking liberties unimaginable to these scarred people would rob them of their dignity.

And so, I didn't open the gate.

I just stood there for a long time, quietly memorizing the scene. The dirt lanes. The few old-fashioned Russian houses—the isbas, unchanged since Czarist times. The abandoned train station.

Finally I had to move on, and we returned to Marusia's house. I drank her tea, ate her apples. I told her about her son Oleg, who had not been back since the train stopped running several years earlier. Marusia and Efim asked me nothing about America; it was too far removed from their experience. They accepted a few trinkets and, in parting, each one kissed me three times in the familial old Russian way.

As for me, I left Russia with a small bag of dirt, a memento for my father and uncle of this place that once held all we were.

I brought it back to our new homeland.

6 IRRESISTIBLE INDIA

"The ATM is right across the street?"

I am at the concierge stand of the Taj Hotel in Mumbai, talking to a gorgeous young man in a snappy uniform.

"Yes, madam. Let me get you car."

"I can walk."

The characteristic smiling horizontal nod reminds me where I am.

"The car is complimentary, madam. I arrange it with manager."

"But the ATM's just across the street?"

"Much traffic, madam. I arrange car."

Soon I am in a beautiful black limo. The driver tells me how wonderful Mumbai is, and that the traffic is minimal because yesterday, January 26, was a huge holiday.

"Everyone new clothes, madam. And Prime Minister. Very big day!"

He reaches for his glove compartment and pulls out a paper flag of India. "For you, madam. Indian Independence Day!"

If this is low traffic, I hate to think of the alternative. We pull out onto a road that seems to have informal lanes in all directions. The sidewalk is chopped up, with the usual bazaar-like scene of bright displays extending over its edges. Tuk-tuks compete with busses. People ten deep wait for transport.

We arrive at the ATM.

I step out of the car, climb over a ditch, and use my card to enter a glass chamber with a Chartered Bank ATM. Moments later the ATM gives me my rupees and a receipt that confirms my balance in a small-town branch of a U.S. bank.

On the street, Western clothes, saris, *salwar kameez*, and black burkas mingle with skinny male legs wrapped in white dhotis incongruously reminiscent of huge diapers and Gandhi. It is pleasantly warm and humid. I wish I had airy light cotton to wear.

When I get back in the car, I ask the driver not to go anywhere. I want to just sit and watch life swirl around us.

The driver points across the road at some nondescript shops and tells me that middle-class people live above them. Then he points to some heavily barred balconies and windows on what might pass as subsidized housing at home.

"The wealthy live there," he says.

"There?"

"Oh, yes," he affirms. "Those are private flats."

"And those bars are for safety?"

"Yes, madam. Very safe, Mumbai, very safe. All people very good in Mumbai."

In response to his question on the drive back across the street, I confirm I am American.

"Ah, America!" he extols. "Is wonderful country, yes? Everyone in America happy, yes?"

"It is a wonderful country, but not everyone is happy. Is everyone in your country happy?"

"Oh, no," he says. "No, some problems, same here, too."

"Do you have car?" he ventures. I am transported to Russia, circa 1977, and a previous conversation about my car.

"I do," I reply.

"For your own self, madam?"

"Yes, for myself. Do you have a car?"

"Oh, no, madam, I have no car." He laughs, as if it were a very funny question. Then he wonders, "And do you have driver?"

It's my turn to laugh. "No, in America it would be very expensive to have a driver. A car is less expensive than a driver."

"Oh," he beams at me. "For 15,000 rupees you can have good driver, madam." He is offering his services, for $250 a month.

We pull up to the security check at the hotel.

"You come back, you ask for Ajay, madam. I take you best shopping in Mumbai. Good shopping in Mumbai. No shopping in Goa. You come back."

I had just arrived in Mumbai, en route to a photography trip to Goa and Kerala, in the south of India. Unbeknownst to me, I was about to learn a lot from the entertaining drivers who moved through traffic like bumper-car heroes. The man who took me to the Mumbai hotel from the airport told me he was from Bangalore.

"But aren't most people moving in the other direction?" I asked about this high-tech hub city of several million.

He shook his head and laughed. "Yes, they are. But we left in 1980. It was just a village then."

Today San Francisco looks much like it did in 1980. But what was a village in the south of India has become a high-tech metropolis in the interim. Even so, I am traveling to that very same region to see nearly naked people with painted skin dance to the gods and elephants parade, just as they have since long before Yerba Buena was occupied by Europeans. It is these contrasts that keep pulling me back to this place, which insinuates its way into the part of you that seeks "the answers to life's persistent questions," as Garrison Keeler would say.

A few days later, I'm in Goa.

The beach stretches into forever. If I had the time, I could walk barefoot the eighty kilometers to the regional capital. I decide on a shorter morning walk, no camera. My beach walk the night before was great, but not very interesting photographically.

I come upon an old black Goan fishing boat. Men drying, mending, and gathering a kilometer's worth of nets. Just my luck! Grateful for my iPhone, I excitedly catalog the fishermen. A black buffalo enters my field of vision, chased by a skinny man in a white dhoti. I am so engrossed in the scene that I fail to notice the buffalo poop—until my feet are covered in it. Fortunately, there's an ocean to clean them in.

Later I discuss the buffalo episode with another driver.

"Very holy, buffalo, very holy!"

"Do they give milk?" I ask, surprised, wondering at the cause of his reverence.

"Oh, no, cow milk better."

"I saw a man chasing a buffalo on the beach."

"In training, madam, in training that buffalo was."

"Training for what?"

"For buffalo fighting, madam."

"Really! When does that happen?"

"Very early in morning madam."

"Can we go see it tomorrow?"

"Oh, no, madam, cannot go see. Very illegal. Need to bribe police. Many rupee."

As I struggle to imagine holy buffalo locking horns, he explains, "Fight finish when one buffalo runs away."

Reluctant warriors, I think.

We pass a tea shop with a sign in big Russian letters. Goa is full of Russians, the driver tells me.

"Very hard," he says. "Russians not speak English. Russian similar to Tamil."

I absorb this startling piece of linguistic information.

"I speak Russian," I offer. The driver says nothing more.

At dinner with two women, one European and the other American, I get an earful.

"The Russians are all loud, fat, and get into fights all the time. According to the drivers that is," says the European, as the American nods affirmatively.

"My Russian father and his brother were tall, slender, and handsome," I say.

I had to admit, however, that we were surrounded by big people speaking loudly in Russian. One man at the front desk was shouting in heavily accented English about the quality of the service.

"They all have those upturned noses, and no one ever smiles," sneers the European, not caring about any cultural sensitivities I might feel.

"My nose is upturned!" I say.

They assure me it's not true—that my nose is not upturned—as if acknowledging any link with the mob of

Russians would be mortifying.

It's a relief to travel and not be greeted as the "ugly American." But did the replacement have to land so close to home?

At breakfast the next morning, while waiting for my fried duck eggs, I turn to the young woman next to me and confirm that, as her accent suggests, she is Russian.

"Why are there so many Russians here?" I ask in her language.

"We wonder why there are so many snooty British!" she replies dismissively, happy to speak her mind. "And aren't you Russian?"

I explain my Russian parentage, and we make peace. I learn it's a seven-hour direct flight from St. Petersburg, and that this hotel is known for not destroying babies' stomachs.

That afternoon I take a drive around the Goa countryside with a local driver the hotel recommends. They make sure I have his cell phone number.

"Do you get good reception here?" I ask. Everyone has a cell phone, but I am having trouble connecting.

"Oh, no, madam," replies the driver. "Cell phone reception very poor. Goan people believe cell phone towers very dangerous."

"Really? Do you believe that?"

"Oh, yes, madam, many children sick. Goa people make government remove cell phone towers."

"So you all have a cell phone, but you do not want cell phone towers."

"Yes, madam. Cell phone towers dangerous. At my house coconuts once very big. Now small. And have stripes." He shakes his head.

"And it's because of cell towers?"

"Yes, coconuts small only near towers. And only after towers arrive."

"Then what do you do with your phones?"

"Oh, madam, we go outside and shout. When phone rings, everyone run quickly."

"In America, some people think holding a cell phone near your head causes cancer," I offer.

The driver heaves a sigh of relief. "Oh, yes, madam, very true, very dangerous."

"So what do you do?"

"We hold phone far from face and shout louder!"

Early the next morning, I wander down the beach again and find David, a Brit, helping my fishing gang collect the net for stowage. He spends two months a year here and has been conscripted as a volunteer.

"They need the help badly," he explains. "The captain stepped on a catfish and didn't treat the injury. Now it's infected and he needs surgery. Xavier," he says, pointing to the man sewing the net in yesterday's photo, "is over eighty, and it's hard to get everything done, shorthanded as they are."

I learn that the group's thirty-year-old black boat, made of slats of wood sewn together, is coated with oil from cashew-nut husks. It is rowed by thin bamboo oars with round Frisbee-like disks at the ends. A crew of up to eight owns the nets cooperatively and goes out daily. They leave around midnight and return, depending on the fish, around five or six in the morning. They immediately stretch the net out to dry, then go have breakfast. They return to mend the nets and, after they are dry, they roll them up in the bottom of the boat, finishing a little before noon. This net is around eight hundred meters long and three meters wide, with floats on one side and stones on the other.

The boats can only go out 500 meters, both by law and because the nets aren't wide enough to go any deeper. The stones drag along the bottom, the net encircles the fish and crabs and shrimp, and brings them in.

"Yesterday was a great day. They got one hundred baskets of anchovies. Today only five baskets of mackerel. It used to be more productive, but now you see those trawlers sitting offshore?" David points to a line of ships in the distance. "They can stay out twenty-four hours and have electricity and sonar to find the fish. So, they get most of the catch. And these guys' sons don't want to fish. This is the end for this kind of work."

"How old are the nets?"

"They repair them, trying to make them last. But basically they have to be replaced every year."

"What do the sons do?"

"They try to get jobs on cruise ships or move to the city. This work is too hard for them."

As we talk, a young man comes up to see if I want to go parasailing or join a dolphin-watching cruise. I take a pass.

I take a closer look at the fishing boat. It is about six feet tall, maybe forty feet long, curved at the bow, a rounded vee at the bottom. There is no machinery of any kind on it. The slats are tied together with a cross-stitch, the symmetry creating the only ornamentation other than a tiny face at the prow. The boat sits on the sand way above the high-tide mark.

When the boat comes in and the nets are still full, a host of sea eagles, terns, and crows dive-bomb the area for easy pickings. Crabs are painstakingly unwound from the netting, fish sorted by type. The mackerel are taken to dry in the sun, destined to end up in a fish curry. The anchovies are washed and poured into large buckets.

By early afternoon it all looks like an abandoned stage set. When I first walked this beach, in fact, I had assumed these craft were long since abandoned, relics from another time.

I thank David, say goodbye to Xavier and the others—noting that they, too, have Portuguese Christian names—and finish my final walk on this wonderful beach of squeaky silver sands.

I sink deeper into India as we move into the countryside, where carts pulled by oxen—horns gaily decorated—exceed automobiles by a good percentage. The men here mostly wear dhoti, surprising me with how young some of them are. I am used to only the elders dressing this way. The light-white cloth glows in the sun against their dark skin. Most have that sinewy leanness I associate with the dress.

We stop on the road to visit with a group of nomads, *Kurbas*, whose family is tending their goats on farmland between crops. They get paid for living there; or rather, their goats do, fertilizing as they defecate. The herd of 2,000, worth up to 2,000 rupees or $40 a piece, makes the nomads quite well off. Although they could sell out and live a middle-class existence in town, they maintain their peripatetic lives, sleeping with their animals on carefully chosen parcels of land.

The road is one lane wide with dirt on each side, everyone moving out of the way for oncoming traffic. In the town we are visiting, Badami, the government has decided to widen the road. Half the town has built their homes right next to it, apparently on public land. So, all the houses are rudely torn in half, leaving exposed walls and piles of rubble. Work goes on and life proceeds as if nothing out of the unusual were occurring.

There is an accepting way here of dealing with the hardballs life throws at you. It would stun the average lawyer-wielding American threatened with their personal liberty or property. It is seen everywhere, although never more than on the roads, where chaos reigns but anger is almost never seen or heard. Instead, trucks have "honk please" painted on their fenders. Honking is used to inform a driver of your presence, as opposed to expressing anger or frustration. It helps you sink into this world if you understand that, if you can accept everything going on around you with curiosity.

One day we climb hundreds of stairs to a fabulous ancient Hindu temple. An orange-robed monk not much bigger than the toes of the giant statue behind him performs rituals involving little Aladdin lamps and flames. Nearby a loin-clothed man washes copper and silver dishware in a soapy tub. Believers kneel to get the monk's blessings and a dab of oil on their foreheads.

I pause to take a picture of four women in beautiful saris coming down some steps. As they pause and smile at me, several men join them.

The women, looking like beautiful butterflies, merge with the plainly dressed, middle-aged men. The men display bored, stern countenances, as if posing for an old-time family portrait. One of my friends joins us, and we gamely click and show our subjects the results. They are thrilled.

I, however, am not. I am determined to grab a few more shots of the butterflies.

Solo.

Ragamuffins are easy to shoo off after showing them a quick pic of their laughing faces. These men are a bigger challenge. They are oblivious to their own drabness. It's as though in their minds they are handsome heroes, at whom we, as mere women, should feel fortunate to point our cameras.

One of the women picks up on the issue and gets the men out of the frame. When we are done with pictures, a conversation ensues.

It turns out that the woman is in charge of a group of visiting schoolteachers.

"How is your society different from ours?" she asks. No

casual chitchat for her.

The thought of representing my entire culture makes me uneasy, all the more so given that we're climbing stairs! I do my best. So does she. The conversation—sharing our experiences as women in our respective societies—opens a door, just a little, into each other's worlds. We embrace like old friends before going our separate ways.

Much like the teacher who wants to understand America, my friends try to understand what it is about India that attracts me. "You're off to India again?" they ask. "What is it that keeps pulling you back?"

As I consider the question again and again as we travel throughout the country, one particular image stands out.

A young woman walks past a background of bright pink, in which an elfin seductress is depicted flirting with some magic, horned white animal. The young woman merges with the background, her diaphanous gown flowing behind her, her long dark hair pulled back, pink seraglio pants reaching jeweled sandals on her feet.

Big deal, one might think. So you hired a model to recreate some Bollywood fantasy. You could have done that in Los Angeles.

In the U.S., the woman might have been mistaken for a prom queen. In reality, I took her photo from our bus as we drove through a primitive village in the countryside. The background image was painted on a pink bus that happened to pass at just the right time. The seductress likely represented Vishnu or one of the other, too-numerous-to-count Hindu gods.

When I took the photo, there were no paved roads other than the one we were driving on. A cart pulled by oxen was just as likely as anything else to be my next image. She, the pink nymph, without a doubt lived in a house with no running water. She would walk with her three-gallon plastic container on her head to the communal water pump. Her outfit would be the same one I had seen her in, and it would not stand out from those of other women in gold and red and blue floor-length saris, laughing and gossiping as they filled their water containers.

If I asked to take her picture, she would probably pose or grab her child to make sure I got him also. When I went to thank her, she would thank me first. If we were near her home, she might invite me in. Her mother would offer me tea.

It is three in the morning when the headless body of a chicken flops next to the crowd. Frenzied drumming and dancing has been going on for hours. I watch a dark-skinned man, face painted, dressed in an elaborate gold and red costume, slit the throat of a chicken.

The ritual turns the man—an untouchable the rest of his life—into a god for a day.

On the grounds of a Hindu temple in a small village in Kerala, I am surrounded by beautifully saried women and children in elaborate finery. Their bold colors contrast with the men, who, even at this festive event, seem drab, dressed mostly in white *lungis*—floor-length shawls tied at the waist—and Western shirts.

Dawn starts lighting the sky, but the line of believers waiting to be counseled by the new god continues to grow. He holds his palm on their foreheads, and they quietly converse for several minutes at a time, their expressions deeply serious. I ache with the desire to understand even one short conversation. It is not to be. This is not some event held for tourists. It is an annual rite, called Theyamm, held in villages all over Kerala. The participants clearly believe in the sanctity of the ritual.

The seemingly unshakable layers of the caste system will return tomorrow. The untouchable might cross the street to avoid sullying the path of a Brahmin. But for these few hours, somehow, the death of a chicken and the elevation of the lowest order of man into a god are mysteriously linked.

Like so many things in India, it is at once intense, mysterious, and—for that one moment—completely credible.

My travel companions and I are welcomed with open arms and warm smiles, asked where we're from, and shown a lack of concern that stuns me for the intrusion of our cameras. The festivalgoers even allow us to film the detailed painting of the god-to-be's face, while he is still untouchable.

The complexities and challenges of life in this constantly astonishing country are far beyond my ability to judge. I am simply grateful for my opportunities to observe and attempt to record my experiences here, convinced it will soon all bow to the normalization that we call the modern world, the one that I come home to in between trips.

There is no easy answer to why India is so irresistible. Its complex messiness and intensity can drive you mad if you don't relax into it. But scene by scene, moment by moment, it works its way into a place deep within you, a place where you never expected to carry the memory of a dark, sinewy, skinny male leg clad in a giant translucent white cotton diaper; a baby frightened to screams by your smiling white face; a ceremonial elephant sharing the road with rush-hour traffic; or a cell-phone-toting *sadhu* in fluorescent orange rushing to an appointment. And echoing back from that deep repository that might be your mind but is more likely your soul, comes a need to see and feel and remember more of those moments.

So you go back. And you find more.

And you know for sure that, given the opportunity, you will go back again, if only to confirm that it's all still there.

Irresistible India.

TANIA ROMANOV

7 TWO NOMADS, THREE CAMELS

A male voice softly chants in prayer to Allah. Wood-smoke aromas tease my nose. Delicate light caresses my eyelids. A firm but forgiving surface holds my weight. One sense at a time, eyes last, a hidden conductor's baton leads me from a dream into a mystery. Where am I?

An old Moroccan proverb says that a good storyteller turns ears into eyes. On that journey I thirsted for so much more. I sought words and memories that would turn my very body into a repository of feeling and emotion. I craved something that could recreate, at my will, those experiences and those moments—undiluted by either time or absence—more personally than any story or filmstrip. My husband, Harold, was slowly leaving me, his cancer continuing an inevitable progression.

We were trekking through the Moroccan Sahara—a nearly empty expanse of dunes, larger than our fifty states—accompanied by three camels and two nomads. Hassan and Mohammed cared so attentively for us in those desert camps that we felt like cosseted elders. They treated us with grace and dignity, catering to needs we didn't even know we had. We developed a hunger for their stories, as they did for ours. The lack of a common language was no barrier to our perpetual curiosity about lives diverse in every way. Hassan and I spent hours communicating reasonably well in French, translating into English and Arabic for Harold and Mohammed.

Hassan and Mohammed both walked with the camels, moving considerably faster than the pace set by Harold. He had learned, by then, the value of moments savored over goals achieved. This left the two of us to follow tracks and find our way alone in this vast uninhabited world. It added an unexpected but delicious tension. We learned that no one ever truly knew our path, for Saharan sands blow themselves new maps so quickly that no cartographer can keep up. We knew the intimacy of sharing a landscape unique in the universe—one that would disappear, erasing all tracks of our presence as soon as we moved on.

Our first night out, we sat on cushioned blankets around the fire: crusty bread emerged from an ingenious oven of ancient nomadic design; couscous and lamb tagine were spiced with a mix blended by Hassan's mother, perhaps handed down through generations of Berber women. He didn't know the French words for the ingredients, but I tasted cloves and coriander, and something fruity and sweet kept us mopping with bread until it was all gone.

When it was time to retire for the night, Hassan walked Harold and me to our private tent, set up between two tall dunes behind the ropes of the dining canvas. After we climbed back with the help of a flashlight, Hassan left us in complete privacy.

Before us stood a basic pup tent. When he squeezed in, my six-foot-six-inch tall husband had to snake like a question mark along the diagonal, not without risk of tearing the seams. There was no room for me, no matter how tightly we normally enjoyed snuggling.

I suggested Harold join the boys in the dining pavilion.

Alone, with the flap tightly zipped, I listened to night noises: roaming, blowing, slithering. Just before we had left on the trip, someone had kindly told me all about the desert horned viper.

I swore it would be my last night alone.

However, sharing a sleeping space with two young Muslims—for there was only the one large comfortable tent—wasn't something I could reconcile with my concept of a world influenced by sharia law. I was old enough to be the young men's grandmother. All the same, their nubile youth transported me back to thirty years earlier, to times sneaking away with Harold in his blond-haired virility.

Even after the first rays of the sun emerged, I waited. Hassan was saying his morning prayers. Only when he finished, did I approach.

"*Hassan, je n'étais pas comfortable seule...*" I started, hesitantly.

"*Ah oui, Madame.* Mohammed and I worried about you all night. We heard the camels snorting, the wind pushing at your tent."

Before I finished washing my face, the young men had moved my bag near the sumptuous set of blankets that took up one corner of the dining tent. Harold used a body language that would evolve over the next days to assure the young men they could sleep in the far corner. They had no interest in either the pup tent or the vipers, and the dark ensured privacy.

Our trip proceeded in calm December weather, the sun warming rather than burning our skin. Nights were cool enough for jackets. Hassan scaled tall dunes during our treks to make sure we weren't heading off for Algeria. Harold and I were welcomed with tea and warm smiles when we reached camp, just as every morning Mohammed greeted us with bedside coffee. And both men adored Harold. They treated him as a beloved grandfather and ached for knowledge of life in America, all three talking every night long past a reasonable bedtime.

Hassan's family was moving to the town of Merzouga, so he could improve his French and go to school for a few years. Mohammed was still living a nomadic life. He guided when opportunities came up.

"How do you know when there is a job?" Harold asked him.

"The company has given me a cell phone!" The pride in Mohammed's voice survived two translations.

"Ah! I'm surprised there's cell phone reception here in the remote desert," Harold remarked.

"There isn't," Mohammed replied.

I paused before translating Harold's next question.

"So what do you do with the cell phone?"

Apparently, the cell phone was an object of great prestige but almost no utility. Word of work was passed on to camel herders, who passed it to nomads at watering holes, who passed it to someone in Mohammed's extended family. In a few days it would reach him.

Hassan and Mohammed were tremendously interested in the subject of marriage.

"How many wives do you have?" Hassan eventually asked Harold, when he realized I would translate anything and not take offense.

"Well, only one," he grinned, "but I was married once before."

They told us their own fathers each had multiple wives.

"So how many wives will you have?" asked Harold. We knew a recent law dictated monogamy, but didn't know how seriously it was being taken.

"Oh, I will have only one!" affirmed Hassan.

"Me too!" exclaimed Mohammed. "If our fathers had to deal with today's independent women, there's no way they could have managed more than one!"

One afternoon I was wandering alone when I spied our group sitting on top of a giant red dune. They were unaware of my approach, concentrating on each other, lots of miming going on. The discussion, I later learned, centered on camels.

On this trip, we were the guests, the camels were the overlords. They carried large loads of goods to feed and shelter us for the journey, and it was their needs that our daily schedule accommodated.

Fortunately, making life easy for the camels worked quite well for us. They could not walk for long in deep sand, so we wove our way through the *wadis*—the dried, flat mud-beds between the dunes. The camels would walk from early morning until around one in the afternoon, then take a break for the rest of the day. Harold now needed that sort of schedule, much more relaxed than our earlier Himalayan treks.

We arrived in camps that were already set up—lunch ready and waiting—and did little for the rest of the day, until the dunes glowed dark red then merged into the night sky.

Now, sitting on top of the dune with Hassan and Mohammed, Harold was writing in the sand with his finger. Mohammed knew a loaded camel could walk twelve kilometers a day, but couldn't translate that into how far we would walk on this trip. They simply didn't think of distances that way. Harold switched from Arabic numbers to a form of Roman numerals to mark twelve kilometers in each of five rows. They got the answer.

"We will walk more than sixty kilometers!" Hassan told me proudly in French, as I walked up to join them.

Those young nomads were experts on life in a place where Harold and I would have no chance of surviving. They knew how to find their families in the remote, changing desert no matter how long they had been gone; how to survive in a climate as arid and dry as any on Earth; how far the camels could walk before they needed water, and how to reach it in time; and, how to bake bread in the wilderness with neither an oven nor matches to start a fire.

In this desert, it was Harold and I who were naïve. Hassan and Mohammed were the wise men.

Soon after our trip, Hassan planned to attend school for the first time. It would be a religious madrasah, one of many set up by Muslim clerics to teach sharia law along with mathematics. The gentle soul I knew might be left behind as he moved into that life. He would perhaps never sleep in the same room with a white woman again, and maybe not with any woman outside his family. I would never sleep in that desert again with my husband—and certainly not in the same tent as two young nomads. But I would always cherish the memories of the time when I did.

Early morning sun projects moving shadows—as in an old-time movie—onto the wall of light canvas before me. A slender, robed figure prostrates itself several times. A camel turns and stumbles away, its front legs hobbled together with a piece of frayed jute. Moments later, new sounds emerge. Metal on rock; a spoon clinking; something rustling.

The smell of coffee mingles in, just as I feel warm skin—which I know as intimately as my own, but will soon lose to his cancer—embrace my curved back. I snuggle close.

Cool air enters with a shaft of light and, through a brief opening in our shelter, red dunes are outlined against blue sky. I observe the vague outlines of the space, more pavilion than tent. A young man, skin dark against his white robe, walks towards us. He kneels silently, sets down a tray with two cups of coffee and some cookies, then heads to the far corner, out of my field of vision.

As Harold idly rubs his hand over my hip in a familiar gesture that says he has awakened, I close my eyes.

I will every membrane of my body to capture this moment.

8 BEHIND THE FACADE

Habana Vieja, Old Havana, you feed my never-ending search for hidden spaces as few others can. Dark doorways, decaying bricks, broken tiles, moldy corners: I am seduced. I venture behind your collapsing walls, I roam through your arched entrances. I cross thresholds of mystery and climb stairs into darkness.

Your ruins are not abandoned; they surge with life.

Why do your crumbling relics entice me? Why do I overcome hesitation and venture into spaces others would think twice to enter? What am I looking for? Who am I seeking?

I walk the streets of a city where many buildings are virtually collapsing onto themselves. A city that, in the end, is the product of a revolution gone wrong—a revolution that holds a key to my connection with this place.

The twentieth was a century of revolutions. Deeply resonant to me are the Russian Revolution, the Yugoslavian Revolution and, finally, the Cuban Revolution—the one that survives to this day. All of them sought to overthrow governments that fostered inequality.

Each resulted in dictatorships.

Two of them had very personal consequences for my family.

My father fled the Russian Revolution as a child, grew up in Serbia, and then was exiled again after the Yugoslavian Revolution, when I was an infant.

Because he was forced to flee, I spent my young childhood in a refugee camp and the rest of my life in the United States. My father regretted his forced flight almost as much as I thanked the universe that we landed in a country that gave me the opportunity to succeed beyond any of his expectations. An opportunity—as I learned over the years—not available to my family who remained in the old country.

In Habana Vieja I was seeing firsthand the consequences of that third revolution. Consequences that inevitably brought to mind memories of visiting Russia and Yugoslavia during the Communist years. Consequences that made me consider how different my life would have been had my father not been forced to flee.

I was searching for what lay behind the decaying facades. Again and again I walked through the neighborhood. Faded blue, green, and cream walls of period buildings; people sitting and chatting on doorsteps; aromas announcing fresh-bread hawkers; ropes lifting produce to old ladies on aging balconies.

On my third day, instead of passing by doorways I had thus far eyed with cautious reserve, I gave into an instinct that had been tugging at me relentlessly.

I was trepidatious as I crossed the first arched threshold. To my right, just beyond the entrance, another crumbling arch opened onto a courtyard, a space filled with abandoned furniture and clothes hung out to dry. To my left, a once-grand staircase rose into the unknown. I silently inched my way back toward the destruction on the other side of the arch.

Having ventured too far inside to have any hope of a quick escape, I heard footsteps rushing down the staircase. I froze. Mesmerized, I beheld dark, glowing skin emerge from the obscurity. A large man flew toward me. Before I had a chance to think what to say or do, he saw me and stopped, startled.

The rebuke I feared didn't come. Instead, the man smiled, wished me a *buen día*, a good day, and continued out the doorway.

A woman came in from the street with a loaf of bread. Her eyes unperturbed as they met mine, she walked past me through the crumbling courtyard. On the other side of it, she walked into a tiny doorway under the stairs, a doorway I couldn't possibly imagine led to a habitation—but apparently did.

A little further down the street, I explored what was once a grand seven-story palace but now brought to mind images of war-torn cities. The grandeur wasn't fading so much as it was disintegrating, makeshift measures in place to save it from total destruction. Frayed wires hung randomly about. Gaping holes in walls eliminated any notion of privacy.

In a hidden corner on the third floor, a middle-aged woman with frizzy red hair responded to my smile and extended hand by introducing herself as Estrella. She invited me into her home for coffee.

Her husband Mario sat watching TV in a room the size of a walk-in closet. We all three snuggled on little chairs that barely fit in the room—mine halfway under the sink.

Afterwards, on my way out of the building, I couldn't resist climbing up to the next floor. As I did, I briefly saw my new friends—back in their chairs across the open central courtyard—through a hole in a crumbling wall that seemed a nudge short of collapse.

Ferocious barking exploded from above. A large dog burst out of an apartment, snarling, lunging at me, then retreating. The noise reverberated through the cavernous openings in the walls. Memories of being bitten in Cuzco a few years earlier paralyzed me. I knew the dog's jaws would reopen the scar on my calf if I were to turn and flee. But what was my alternative?

I held the dog's eyes as I slowly backed down the stairs.

But he sensed my fear and was emboldened by it.

Suddenly, Estrella's shout penetrated the din. The dog cowered and backed off, his owner emerging to further calm him down. The dog owner and Estrella—clearly good friends—chatted briefly, and peace was restored.

"Take more photographs," Estrella said on the way back to her room, as she leaned through another opening in a wall. "Please!"

I pointed the camera at her for a final image. We exchanged a few more phrases, and then I wished her good luck. She beamed and wished me the same. I noted her address, along Habana Street, and vowed to return the next day.

The dog was quickly forgotten, but the interactions between neighbors stayed with me as I walked back for breakfast at the *casa particular* where I was staying. Tight quarters, open doors, windows lacking glass, no privacy—life lived in the public square. These people might as well have been trapped in an enormous traffic jam for the last sixty years, but there was no road rage evident. Instead, there was a warmth and mutual regard that let them smile openly when a complete stranger entered their world.

It was the kind of warmth that my father missed for years after he fled his Belgrade of the 1950s, around the same era that Havana was still trapped in today. He bemoaned his morning bus rides to work in San Francisco, where passengers kept to themselves. How, he wondered, could they see the same faces daily and yet remain strangers? Where was the warmth and jocularity he so craved?

As a child I didn't understand what it was that he so missed. Why, I wondered, couldn't he just fit in? Why couldn't he be like other fathers? But these people in Havana were giving me insight into my father's past, mirroring it a continent away. Perhaps San Francisco felt as foreign to him as this environment did to me.

Later that day, I entered another narrow courtyard. A woman I had smiled at on the street reached out to me. She noticed my Japanese-American friend Linda, then pointed at herself. As she repeated *"Chino,"* we weaved back to her rooms. There, she pointed to a portrait of her father, hanging in the upper corner of the room, the same spot filled in my father's living room by an Orthodox icon. Her father was handsome and looked part Chinese. Clearly it was a heritage of which she was proud.

Linda and I returned a few days later. We learned to spell her name—Carlixta Gómez—from her ration booklet, since she did not know how to read or write. She still used that ration book—thirty years after the death of the Soviet Union, whose version it was modeled on—to get the rice, beans, and cooking oil that supplemented her fifteen-dollar monthly pension.

Again I started making comparisons to my family's past. I looked around and imagined Yugoslavia as it must have been during my youth in the States, the old country my father couldn't let go as I grew to adulthood in my adopted home. What if my parents hadn't left Serbia? What if I hadn't grown up in a refugee camp? What if I weren't an American?

In my childhood, although by American standards we were still quite poor, every three months my mother sent each of her five sisters in Yugoslavia a much-needed care package of powdered eggs and milk and food in dented cans.

What if?

The first time I visited Yugoslavia, as a college student, I learned that six of my cousins had shared one bed in the only room in their apartment other than the tiny kitchen—a bed I was sharing with the youngest ones who still lived at home.

What if?

Here in Habana, what if these dark spaces I was now exploring had sheltered me instead of these Cuban people?

This is the litany that plays in my mind. This is the fear that won't let go, the dark place I need to explore.

So I wander the streets and enter the shadowy spaces,

looking to reconcile my present with my past.

When my young cousin comes from Serbia and wishes he could figure out—in these days of intense immigration repression—some way to stay in America, I wonder: why me?

When I learn another cousin in Belgrade sleeps downstairs in the winter because she cannot afford to fix the leak in her roof, I wonder: why me?

When I walk into dark ruins in Havana and meet a grinning woman who offers me coffee in her closet-sized hovel, I wonder: why me?

Shifting between the torment of *what if?* and *why me?* I reach out to those I come across. I share a smile, some caring words, my respect. For their strength and their brave acceptance of reality, I would give them my tears.

A few days later, I went back to see Estrella and take her a trinket from San Francisco. This time I strode confidently through the arched doorway. I was entering a friend's home. I eyed the floral patterns of the metal art-deco banisters on the stairway, the fading grandeur of warm-toned plaster of paris. I stepped over broken beams and past chips of stucco.

I met Estrella's daughter, who lived next door, along a perilous walkway. I told her how her mother had saved my life from the ferocious dog. We laughed as neighbors passed on their way out.

My mind returned to a visit with my aunt in Belgrade in 1968. We stood at her back door while neighbors wandered up and down the wooden staircase, stopping to chat. The casual, spontaneous interactions felt warm and friendly. I told my aunt how much my father missed that camaraderie.

"Yes, but," she said, "he might not miss it so much if he couldn't escape it, as I can't."

Her reply helped me see that underlying this lifestyle that my father romanticized was a lack of alternatives, poverty and crowding.

And so I am torn between a father forced to flee, who never quite recovered, and a mother who joined her husband in exile but adapted to make America her home. I am torn by my sorrow over the life he left behind, by my grief that I never knew the successful young man who captured my mother's heart.

The crumbling Habana Vieja brings me closer to the truth of my own life. I start understanding what I am seeking. Somewhere in those dark spaces I might even find myself.

What if?
Why me?
Why *not* me?

TANIA ROMANOV

9 MA GANGA

A corpse wrapped in gold foil, tenuously balanced on the shoulders of a group of men, jostled past me. Its bare soles bobbed as they disappeared into the crowded alley leading down to the river. I stared while skirting the cremation *ghats*—burning fires and dense smoke—and barely avoided falling on the twisting cobblestones of Varanasi.

"You don't allow women at cremation rituals here in India because you're afraid they might still throw themselves on the fire?" I asked, as I caught up to Raju, a young Indian I met in my wanderings. I knew the old custom of *sati*, widows practicing self-immolation, had been illegal for years.

"Oh, perhaps it started for that reason," Raju replied, politely oblivious to my cynicism, "but now it is part of our culture. Our brothers, fathers, and husbands perform this sacred ritual."

"And who performed your own good husband's cremation?" Raju continued, not pausing from his effortless weaving through the crowds.

Saved by another jostling corpse from having to give an

immediate response, I stopped to watch a skinny, nearly naked black man weighing large pieces of wood. They were for the pyres that were lit hundreds of times daily in this most holy of places.

I was spending several weeks on *Ma Ganga*—the Mother Ganges river—the heart and soul of India's Hindu culture. For days my group of travelers floated on small boats covered by old cloth canopies, each rowed by two young, gently muscled dark-skinned men wrapped in *lungis*—the six-foot-long cloths that cover most Indian men from the waist down, except in the centers of large cities. Often the banks of the river were quiet, just oxen mingling with night herons, granting an unexpected perspective on this vibrant land. As we floated down the river, moments imprinted themselves like snapshots.

Our small boat gliding along a placid channel, the water pale blue, the sun gentled by constant haze, my two female travel companions and I relaxed against colorful pillows. Our oarsmen lay asleep in the prow while the current did their work for them. Beneath our idle gaze a group of large black birds—crows or ravens—alighted on a body-shaped object floating in the water.

Later, smoke on a rocky, garbage-strewn bank cleared to reveal three sinewy men cremating a young family member. One of the men deftly reached into the fire to pull out shards of bone, throwing them into the river. The men then splashed water onto the flames in what I presumed was the final step of the ritual.

Early one evening, our boats approached our campsite, a broad expanse of sand that formed an island in the post-monsoon river. As I jumped ashore, I had to avoid a round white object. Our oarsman said it was a skull. I was relieved when a fellow traveler laughed and assured me it was just an old piece of Styrofoam.

During the Sonepur Mela celebration in Bihar, near the confluence of the Ganges with the Gandak, we joined over one million people bathing in the river at what was considered a most auspicious moment—the November full moon.

Walking among increasingly dense crowds towards the broad river, I saw a barber snap his scissors overhead. He was advertising his availability to perform children's first-ritual head shavings. Later, since many parents would be unable to reach the river due to the density of the mob, I would see bald babies trustingly passed above the crowd, assuring their dunking before the rising sun flashed on the water.

The Ganges flows for 1,000 miles through India. People aspire to bring their deceased loved ones to sacred spots along its banks, like Varanasi and Haridwar, to assure peace for their souls.

Tourists also flock to Varanasi. At sunset the river is full of twenty-passenger boats rowing up and down between the two large cremation ghats, visitors staring in rapt amazement at the fires. The evening religious ceremony is now performed under glowing neon lights. In a carefully orchestrated performance, seven priests dressed in gold swing flames to loudly broadcasted chants. Prosperous Indians fill the front sections of stands above the stage and, in spite of the strong tourist presence, believers crowd the banks.

Standing above this melee, I watched a hawker entice a baby with a poodle-shaped balloon—the father too polite to chase him away, the hawker intent on getting the child to demand the toy. The whole scene could have fit somewhere between St. Mark's Square and a country carnival.

Wandering off, I came upon a quiet alcove where a holy man was setting up his gratitude ritual. He invited me to sit. In an intensely personal ceremony, he steered my soul to my deceased husband, Harold, welcoming him to the circle of the blessed. I chanted along and tossed bunches of seeds, gripped with my thumb and middle two fingers, onto the fire in time with his rhythm. I left the puja with not only a decorated forehead but a profound sense of peace.

Eventually I headed for the cremation ghats, where work continued into the night. I learned that each body is allocated a large amount of hardwood. The flame is brought from a perpetual fire—lit by Shiva thousands of years ago—and the fee is based on the wealth of the recipient.

The men in a family stay the three to ten hours it takes to complete a cremation, having brought the body on their shoulders through town. The government, concerned about conservation, built a sophisticated modern crematorium. It sat ignored. People wish for their loved ones' ashes to enter Ma Ganga in the traditional way, the ceremony a joyous time in which the soul is freed.

My mind returned to that question Raju had innocently asked: "And who performed your own good husband's cremation?"

I was horrified to realize I had no idea.

Complete strangers took my husband's body away from my home. I later received his ashes in a polished wooden urn I had selected in the sterility of a crematory along the freeway not far from my house.

I suddenly saw my world through the eyes of my Indian hosts.

Their rituals of death, the normality of corpses and skulls, the belief that a river can ease the passage to the afterlife; these are all ways in which people accept the unacceptable, the loss of a loved one. Our ways might seem as impersonal and foreign to them as dead bodies floating in rivers are unimaginable to us. Our horror might be perceived as callous judgment.

The floating object with black birds on it did in fact turn out to be a dead body—a lost corpse. The Styrofoam ball really was a water-smoothed human skull.

I could not leave Ma Ganga unchanged.

When I later shared stories of the trip, questions about dead bodies in the river dominated the conversation, second only to awe over the intensity of the cremations and revulsion over the crowding, filth, and chaos.

Listening, I recognize how much my own perspectives had evolved in India.

An old fear of crowds dissipated. Faith and fantasy came to cohabitate with greater ease in my scientific, Western mind. Death began to harmonize more naturally with life. I knew Harold's spirit now roamed more freely.

Early one morning at my riverside campsite, I watched a holy man appear out of the mist. He roamed alone in a land of a billion people, on his river, oblivious. I carry that scene with me, the memory helping me walk in serenity. From my low angle I saw him effortlessly walk out onto and over the water.

Of course, I thought.

10 ECHOES OF OKUNOIN

Every step took me deeper into the ancient heart of Okunoin, the largest and most revered cemetery of Japan, a shadowy forest of giant cedars and stone markers; of mists and mosses; of ghosts present and past. The trails, hidden under mud and needles, pulled me away from the well-maintained and heavily visited formal areas of pagodas and pavilions. Water dripped from overhead branches. Old stones leaned gently together. I slowed and followed a weak beam of sunlight to a mismatched pair of eroding markers, when a sudden vibration in my pocket interrupted my reverie. *Was someone trying to reach me?*

It was the fall of 2015, and I was staying at a temple in the small mountain town of Koyasan, between visits to Tokyo and Kyoto. Previous travels in Japan, some years ago, had involved my high-tech business career. My time in Japan hadn't started smoothly. The enigmatic politeness I encountered made negotiation challenging. One of the first executives I worked with casually mentioned that women walked two steps behind men in his culture, a comment he would later come to regret, when he learned

I controlled his investment budget. His culture and I never matched wavelengths.

On this return trip, I wanted to see what it felt like to explore freely, without worrying about the next meeting or how to dress for dinner with high-level executives and geishas. In the aftermath of my husband Harold's death, I was exploring different ways to see, learning to appreciate the Zen aesthetic in my life and art. Surely a land where the *wabi-sabi* values of imperfection and naturalness were venerated had much to teach me.

What I didn't know was whether I was open to learning from it.

I wasn't a natural for the subtle courtesies of Japan. My upbringing in a family of immigrants from Russia and the Balkans was raucous and combative. Family members expressed themselves loudly and fervently. I had to work hard to keep my sense of self, to not be overrun by their strong beliefs. I was outspoken and articulate; I shouted loudly and persistently. My writing is still more Tolstoy than Tanka, raw personal exposé rather than symbolic, measured Haiku.

But now I was back in Japan.

I explored.

In Kyoto I had walked the Philosopher's Trail along a creek bed, then veered onto side streets. I visited a pottery collector and unexpectedly found a unique instrument called the *hamon*. Made of rough cast iron and shaped like half of a giant ostrich egg, this simple object, similar to a slit drum, converted my inexpert taps to tones as delicate as water drops in an echoing cavern, a sound that spread like a ripple of water.

In Tokyo I had roamed aimlessly for days, confident because my phone always knew how to get back to my hotel. I walked through glossy department stores selling hundred-dollar mushrooms and marveled at the cleanliness of this city of millions.

Several trains and a funicular had brought me to the mountains. In my mornings in Koyasan, I had explored temples of an austere intimacy. They contrasted radically with the elaborate and vibrant Russian Orthodox cathedral of my youth. Instead of nearly explosive singing in many keys, I heard modulated male voices chanting, their haunting tones escaping into the surrounding fog and forests. Memory and reality mixed and melded.

Now, as I continued deeper into the cemetery, I walked up and down steep hillsides and through giant cedar trees that reminded me of the redwoods of Northern California, where Harold's ashes are scattered.

And then I reached that moment shattered by my phone vibrating.

Resting in my room that morning, I had finished the newest mystery by Louise Penny, a favorite Canadian author. In the final sentences, the protagonist discovers that the name of his newest grandchild is Zora, my mother's name—and one rarely heard outside the Balkans. I pondered the coincidence.

I took out my phone. It was my calendar.

My wedding anniversary. I laughed. Harold and I were so bad at dates that for almost thirty years—in the days before smart devices—it was my mother's phone call that alerted us to the day's significance.

But there was a second reminder.

Tomorrow, September 13, would mark the anniversary of my mother Zora's death.

Everything about the day took on new significance. Harold and my mother had always been extremely close. Evidently my two loved ones were tag-teaming from beyond this world to make sure I remembered them. I don't visit my parents' graves. Yet here I was in a cemetery, and Harold and my mother were using the airwaves to communicate with me. How very Zen, I thought, an uncanny marriage of tradition and technology; of the sublime and the pedestrian; of my high-tech past and my more contemplative present.

Wispy tendrils of mist wafted like the smoke from swinging incense burners at my parents' funerals. I stood before two stone markers—one short, one tall—one lit by the brief sun's glow, one in deep shadow. The pairing was perfect. My six-foot-six-inch-tall husband had towered over me like my father had over my tiny mother. I was in a perfect place, physically and spiritually, to receive and understand my mother's message.

The next grouping I saw engendered my whole family, everyone I had lost, represented by old stones covered with bright-green moss, glowing in the dark, transcending temple and cathedral.

I lost myself on that amazing mountain, walking in silence. In that forest cemetery far from all our homes—past and present—my ancestors had found me. My tears blessed their memories, and I walked for hours in a peace I have rarely found anywhere else, listening to them without fear that they would overwhelm me.

Like baby Zora's arrival near the end of that mystery novel, life continually presents me with unexpected synchronicity and powerful signs. I no longer manage businesses or control investment budgets. The knowledge that we control little beyond ourselves has settled deep within me. My need to shout has moderated greatly, although I know it will never entirely disappear.

In the earlier chapters of my life, I saw the world mostly in black-and-white and was blinded by my need to transform it. Japan showed me that I had changed. I had learned to hear, to see. To just be.

11 ON THE BEACH

In the city of Puri, on the east coast of India, a place of pilgrimage and—more importantly—beaches, I was awake at the 5:30 a.m. light. I decided to head for a walk on the beach, where the sun toyed with a few clouds.

I soon found a bracelet in the sand, a triple band of little brown wooden beads. I asked a handsome young man—the only person in sight—if it was his. He said no and suggested we throw it back into the ocean. Somehow, it became clear that the bracelet was meant to be an offering—to the sea, the sky, the silence.

Some women in saris collected wood along the beach. I snapped a picture of them emerging from the sunrise. I thought we were enjoying a shared moment, until a man walked up and asked for money—on behalf of the women, it seemed.

Most people here enjoyed having their pictures taken and often asked me to take more. A fair number did check, as a fleeting gesture, to see if I had something to give them in exchange. Since I don't give people money to take pictures, when that happens, I just walk away. I have

learned, however, to carry a few San Francisco key chains or postcards as gifts for people I connect with in my wanderings.

As I was returning from my walk, crowds were descending upon the beach. A drone hovered overhead.

Next I came upon a camel, a group of photographers, and two more drones. The photographers told me they were shooting a "preevary"—a short video, they clarified. They also explained that a bride and groom were involved. I spied the couple and walked over to them. They were shooting a "preeveg," they explained.

Eventually I understood they were shooting a pre-wedding video and had flown to the beach just for this photo shoot.

I continued walking and found a group of people who would be considered insane in any other circumstances. They were old and skinny, wearing saris and dhotis. At the direction of their spiritual leader, they fearlessly entered the water and spread themselves facedown on the sand, waiting for the waves. When the waves came, the people were submerged in a broiling mass of bubbles. The stronger women pulled men weighing around sixty pounds—definitely near their last pilgrimage—to their feet and back to shore.

My own gods drove me closer to capture their images. I ran to escape a large wave, getting soaked and almost crashing into a few worshipers on my way out of the water. This continued until they had all finished their ritual. Then they walked toward me, telling me how happy they were.

"Happy! Happy!"

It was either their only word of English, or their joy had wiped the rest of their vocabulary from their minds. I never figured out exactly what they were trying to do, but I assumed it was some sort of religious ritual. The group walked away, and the beach was turned back over to tourists.

I was now soaked, a sandy, salty mess. My grin reached from ear to ear as I returned to my hotel. It was only thanks to the man watering the bushes, who obliged me by spraying off my legs, that I was allowed back inside.

12 PASSAGE IN INDIA

A large Buddha gazes out from his altar in the back of a long dark room. Yak-butter candles flicker, adding a tinge of gold to the pale light coming through the door. Fifty monks in simple wool robes of maroon and saffron sit facing the middle aisle. Their monotonal chants fill the air with a humming that has echoed in these mountains for millennia.

Worlds away, in the heart of San Francisco, smells of incense fill the nave of a large, candlelit cathedral. A Russian Orthodox priest presides, his long, white beard reaching to the gold cross on his chest, his ornate robe brocaded in gilt. Rosy light filters in through stained-glass windows. Mourners stand, as is their custom, while the priest and deacon chant a funeral liturgy in a bass rumble that echoes the Buddhist chanting I listen to 10,000 miles away. My husband and I are trekking through the remote Himalayas of northern India.

It is the summer of my thirty-eighth birthday. The funeral is my father's. My mother, brother, family and friends are there, but weeks pass before I hear of the death not one of us had reason to expect. No premonition, no sense of loss, no interruption in my deepening sense of peace warns me that, in a distant place I have no access to—with a lifetime of our issues unresolved—he is gone. I don't see his face one last time. I don't hear the heavy sound of dirt thrown on his coffin.

By the time I see his grave, grass covers it.

Only at the end of the trip, in the sweltering chaos of New Delhi in August, when I call my mother to confirm our arrival in San Francisco, do I learn my father has died.

In a brief phone conversation punctuated by static, wire delay, and tears, I crumple into a five-year-old, missing my smiling, playful Papa. Papa—the one who called me *Tanichka, Taniusha, Zolotko*, golden child, and an endless collection of loving nicknames—is gone.

I hang up the telephone and cling to my husband, but real grieving doesn't come. I want my mother. I need her strength and support. I need to share our bond of a lifetime of memories of Papa. My feelings are in turmoil. Sadness, anger, and guilt collide with exhaustion. I suddenly loathe New Delhi and must get home.

On my return to San Francisco, instead of the strong parent who raised me, I find a frail old woman whose hair has suddenly turned gray. I must shunt away fatherless little Tania and become the strong daughter my mother needs. Mama is devastated, sad and angry. Worse, she is helpless in a way I have never seen her before. Now is not the time to dwell on my own grief; indeed, I can barely find it.

I learn what it means to have missed my father's funeral. I lost that exquisite moment when I could feel sorry for myself or berate myself for not being the wonderful, loving, perfect daughter my father should have had. I didn't apologize or thank him or cry with those who also loved him. I forfeited the moments when his death was the only thing that mattered, before life started to move into a future in which he would not participate.

A few years later I attended the funeral of Zhenya, a dear lifelong friend, a man I had adored as a child. By then I had long rejected the rituals of the church, the notion of comfort from the indecipherable mumbling of old men with long, white beards in ornate robes, swinging incense lamps. But for those two hours, which once would have meant an eternity of fidgeting, I sobbed without stopping. Yes, Zhenya was dear to me; but it was my father I cried for that day, for the ceremony I missed, and the peace still lacking from my thoughts of him.

Time passed. Life intervened. Closure remained elusive.

And then I once again immersed myself in a long Himalayan trek. High in the mountains, in whose beauty I find my own sacred and personal temple, I had a vivid, joyous dream about my father. He was alive and happy, and I knew with certainty that he loved me. I was back in those beloved mountains, surrounded by deeply spiritual chanting, where I had been when he died. Seeing him again in that setting told me he forgave me for all the turbulent times in our relationship.

When I awoke, the block of ice that had been trapped deep inside me finally started melting away.

NEVER A STRANGER

13 ANGELS AND DEMONS

Saviors and monsters.
 Angels and devils.
 Good and evil.
 Life.
 "How did Lenin turn into a monster?"

Our writing group was critiquing my book about my family's exile from Russia a hundred years ago. Trying to mix personal story with world history is a challenge; but this question had nothing to do with my writing.

I had tried to paint Lenin as neutrally as I could, as a man who started out with the goal of creating a worker's paradise. Just a few pages later he had launched the Red Terror, which eventually evolved into Stalin's genocidal rule. Whatever their initial objectives, the revolutionaries had replaced the Tsar with a far greater evil.

"You know, he's not the only example of a leader trying to bring salvation through communism who instead brought damnation," someone said.

My mind returned to Cambodia, where I had recently traveled. Someone else brought up China. The debate disintegrated into disagreements over Cuba. It was hard to bring the discussion back to my writing.

A few days later a *New York Times* headline announced: *Khmer Rouge's Slaughter in Cambodia Ruled Genocide*. The article continued: "Pol Pot and his communist disciples turned the country into a deadly laboratory for agrarian totalitarianism."

Russia judged Stalin just a few years after his death. Cambodia waited forty years to succumb to external pressure to judge Pol Pot's supporters. A photograph accompanied the story.

Just days earlier I had been hosted by the prison's official photographer at his home in Siem Reap. I met his mother, wife, and child. I documented and photographed our time together.

Nhem En was an enigma. He was completely flat in his affect, and his eyes revealed nothing. He made his living from the world's morbid curiosity about his past.

As I listened to him talk, all I could think about was how my father, too, took pictures of people with an uncertain future. But my father's were photos of those waiting to go to Canada or Venezuela or America. Nhem En's were of people facing certain death.

My father never talked about his time in a refugee camp, his own years of an uncertain future. Nhem En hasn't stopped talking about it for two decades. A few years ago *The Guardian* wrote: "And the photographer is far from a sympathetic advocate: before starting his career as a self-published author, he tried to sell Pol Pot's sandals and toilet seat online."

Cambodia continues to haunt me. My graduation from college, in 1970, was canceled because the University at Berkeley rose up in protest in response to the U.S. invasion. My father was deprived of seeing the result of years of hard work; he was dead by the time my graduation was ceremonially held in 1990.

Cambodia is still recovering. In the declaration of genocide, the tribunal found only three living people guilty. All others have been exonerated of any influence in the decisions taken by the leadership. Lucky for them, since many—including the current prime minister—were Khmer Rouge members.

One of the guilty was named Dhuc. He ran the notorious prison and was Nhem En's boss. Nhem En explained that he testified against Dhuc. And then he dropped what was, for me at least, another bombshell: he had photographed Pol Pot with a Yugoslav leader.

In 1950 Pol Pot had spent a month building a highway project in Yugoslavia. During his rule, Cambodia considered Yugoslavia one of its few friends in the world.

"Wait," I wanted to say. "Leave me out of this!"

I was an infant in Yugoslavia in 1950. I did not need to learn that my mother's country supported this horrific dictator. I had already lived through watching my homeland endure one war crime tribunal. Did it help to reassure myself that it was the totalitarian leader of Yugoslavia who exiled my family?

In any case, I was in Siem Reap to take a photography workshop, not to torment myself. People came here to see the ancient temples of Angkor, not to revisit their past.

A few days later, walking out of the gate from the temple of Angkor Thom, I stopped to photograph some faces on a bridge. They represented a story of guardian gods and demon gods facing off to roil the waters of the Earth.

A thousand years later, it seems the gods are still at war. My personal demons are also still at battle. Once you start turning the pages of your past, I have learned, you can't control what comes out.

14 TENAKEE SPRINGS

An enormous bald eagle startled us as it swooped in to snag the bass that little Sadie had just released.

It was that eagle and all the fish we didn't keep—including the halibut, which, at one hundred pounds, was too large and therefore too tasteless to bother with—that I remember about our fishing exploits in Southeast Alaska. We were not on a fishing expedition, however; but, rather, on an exploration of nature. Three generations of our extended family were spending a week cruising on the teak yacht Discovery. Built in 1931 to host movie stars represented by the William Morris agency, its current owners had lovingly restored it.

My curiosity was piqued when I heard we would be stopping overnight at a particular small town. Tenakee Springs, we were told, had a hundred people in the winter, maybe two hundred fifty during the summer. Given my passion for photographing people in remote places, I couldn't wait to explore the town, which also boasted hot springs and a lodge.

Our captain worried about the constant rainfall on the

first days of our voyage; about the fact that, for the only time in his career, he got skunked halibut fishing; that the whales were missing from their usual haunts; and, that a cruise ship had overtaken his heretofore-secret cove. The ten passengers fretted and wondered what we had signed up for, other than a week of three generations sharing tight quarters.

My thirteen-year-old grandson, Baker, already exceeded six feet and was close to scratching his head on every ceiling. Stella, Sadie, and Alice, young teenagers, were too big to fit into the berth that was supposed to hold four people. My brother and sister-in-law ceded their double, they, too, struggling to fit into the cramped space.

Nature soon distracted us from our difficulties getting settled. Emily filled a pitcher from a giant waterfall that roared as our ship hovered just inches away. A few yards from the boat two humpback whales faced us and opened their vast brown-toothed jaws. We watched a family of orcas kill a sea lion, stretching out the experience as a training exercise for their young one. A black bear stood before us against a rock cliff, licking the salt and perhaps eating the mussels below the high-tide line. He mesmerized us with his skill in working his way up the cliff, transforming himself from a bulky black beast into the replica of a human starting the El Capitan climb in Yosemite.

The weather was as capricious as promised. The sky filled with clouds, rainbows, and sunbows in rapid succession.

On the third afternoon we pulled into Tenakee Springs.

I got off the boat and walked up the dock. As I stepped onto the roughly packed mud I would soon get used to walking on, I entered what could have been a charming grove of firs, if not for a random collection of junk. The only redeeming man-made features were a tattered tire-rope swing and an old phone booth—paint peeling, door ripped off, payphone replaced by a handset.

I pointed my camera at the booth, where a heavyset guy stood in the doorway. He put a can of Coke in front of his face, so I wouldn't take a picture.

When I approached, he told me he was waiting for a phone call. He didn't want to be in a photograph, but he begrudgingly moved out of the way so I could take a picture of the booth.

"Oh my god, there's an old landline here!" I exclaimed.
"Well, duh..." The man rolled his eyes.
"Do you live here?"
"Why else would I be here?"
"I don't live here, and I'm here."
"Well, I'm sorry for you." He turned his back on me.

Before I could react, an overweight woman with a little child and a giant malamute walked up. The child got onto the swing and said "Watch me!"

The woman ignored him.

I moved on, soon distracted by bushes all around me of yellow and red berries. A young lady with a backpack and a grocery bag full of toilet paper walked along the muddy road.

"Excuse me. What are these berries?" I asked.

"I think they're salmon berries," the woman replied.

"So you just eat them? They look sort of like raspberries?"

"I really don't know. I'd have to ask."

"Oh, you don't live here?"

"Yes, but I'm just not into the Berry Thing."

Snubbed again, but with a smile this time, I continued toward town.

I was sure the next group I saw, an older woman and a younger couple, were tourists, just off a boat like I was. I decided to find out.

"Where are you from?" I asked

"We live here," the older woman replied.

"Really? How long have you been here?"

"Two years. We just retired two years ago. We're from Seattle," explained the guy.

The four of us walked up to a tall building that said "Mercantile."

"That's our home," they said.

It looked like something out of an old Western.

"How old is it?" I wondered.

"It was built in 1891. But we remodeled the whole thing extensively."

The group was very friendly, so we kept talking as we wandered up to their door. The front of the building was occupied by the town grocery store. The back had been converted to large glass-fronted rooms with views of the bay. A broad dock led out into the water. We were in the heart of town.

Across the way was another public telephone booth. It made sense, for there was no cell reception in town. A woman sat in the booth.

I walked toward the long pier. On my right was a small museum. It was closed, but a sign said they would open upon request. There was a number to call.

Circling back, I approached the woman in the phone booth and asked her if I could take a picture. I told her I hadn't seen working phone booths in a long time.

"This one definitely works," she said. "The phone was ringing when I walked up."

As we chatted, the heavyset woman from the first phone booth came up to us. I smiled.

"I see you're walking around town taking pictures freely," she said. "Did you take a picture of my child?"

I didn't want to tell her it was the last thing on my mind. Instead, I politely said, "No, I didn't take a picture of either of you. I've gotten everyone's permission before I've taken their picture."

Before the woman could respond, her dog, the giant malamute, tipped over her groceries and started eating a large box of berries. She ran off, screaming at the dog. I continued my conversation with the lovely lady in the phone booth, and didn't see the fat woman again.

The woman in the booth lived part-time in Washington State. In 1989 she bought a cottage on the far side of town and now spent most of their time here. She was waiting in the phone booth because it was next to the bathhouse. Painted with a cute image of a bear and an elk sharing a tub, the bathhouse had separate hours for men and women. My new friend explained that it was not currently the time for women to bathe, and that when they do they're naked.

"Then tourists come and ask if it's all right to photograph us. I ask if they would like us to walk into their bathroom and photograph them."

Farther down the road, a couple walked out of their house. I said hello. They returned my greeting, then paused to warn me that a bear had been marauding around town. They pointed to some crushed brambles heading uphill toward the forest.

Right after, I ran into an old guy with a beard. He was picking berries, and he told me to get the darkest ones, which did in fact taste better than the tart, slightly bitter ones I'd nibbled on earlier.

"You're the first person I've seen eating these berries," I observed.

"Oh my god, we all eat them all the time!"

I asked him if it was OK for an out-of-towner to eat them.

"Well, thank you for asking. Of course it is. Although I

guess it would be in bad taste to bring in a big barrel and take them all home with you!"

The man's name was Brook, and he and his wife had lived in town for thirty years.

"How did you end up here?"

"Well, we are sailors. We were sailing around one year, and we were looking for a place to spend the winter."

"The winter?" I said.

"Yes, the winter." He noticed my skepticism. "It's surprisingly mild here compared to what you might expect. This is not the Arctic."

I moved on, thinking I would be hard-pressed to spend a month in their rainy summer, let alone the winter.

Two more women in raingear came walking towards me. Again, I smiled and said hello.

"Are you from here?" I asked.

"Yes, we are. Welcome!"

"Thank you! I'm enjoying your town—and your berries."

"Enjoy the berries, but not the bears!" I was to hear that joke repeatedly.

"I understand one is on the roam."

"Oh, a lot more than one," one of the women said, pointing at more broken brambles. "One just ran through there yesterday."

"I'm wearing pink," I said. "He'll be sure to see me."

"Yes, but he might take you for a big pink berry!"

Continuing my stroll around town, I ran into my family. They were heading back to the boat. They had finished their exploration faster than me, since they didn't feel a need to talk to every stranger along the way.

I passed the library, one more weathered edifice in a town full of them. Two people sat on the stairs. The library was closed, but just up the road there was a small shack filled with books. It turned out to be a store where everything was free. A notice on the board explained people could leave anything they wanted, but if it was still there two weeks later, they had to take it back. This was not a dump!

Other notices told of Saturday pizza night at the bakery, and that the Tenakee volunteer fire department no longer provided emergency medical care. Lorna was looking for a place to plug in her freezer from April to November, and the fuel dock was open from 10:00 to 2:00, except Tuesdays and Thursdays. I had already learned those were the legal fishing days.

The town meandered along this main road, which could hold a car, but in practice only supported bicycles, ATVs, children's wagons, and feet. I figured it might go on forever and decided to turn around when the rain got more serious and the houses started getting more spread out.

I passed a young lad and his father fishing along the shore. They hadn't caught anything. I wished them good luck.

As I neared the center of town again, I overtook an older guy walking slowly, in a red seafarer's jacket and hat. He greeted me and said, "How you doing?"

"I'm great. How about you?"

He walked on for a while, pondering my question.

"I'm tired." His pace slowed further yet.

A woman on a white bicycle, whom I had already passed several times, rode toward me. I stopped to give her room to pass. Before she reached me, she pointed to some hidden stairs, smiled, and said, "I'm going up this way. I am done for the day. Time for my nap."

I, too, was ready for my nap.

On my walk through Tenakee Springs, I had met over a third of the residents, the population currently closer to fifty than a hundred, not only the lodge, but many houses for sale. Giant black slugs considerably outnumbered people, as I suspect had always been true.

The last person I passed was the phone-booth curmudgeon, who now sheepishly smiled. It turned out his call had come in, and his mood seemed greatly improved by it.

My mood was greatly improved, too, by a couple of hours in Tenakee Springs.

15 SAN FRANCISCO STORYTELLER

I don't normally take a cab home from the writers' group, but it's late and cold. So, I run to the St. Francis Hotel, knock on the window of a minivan taxi, and climb in back.

I ask the baby-faced older man if he takes credit cards.

He says a brusque "yes" and pulls away from curb.

I immediately think, "He's Russian." But he is determinedly silent. Neither that one word nor anything particular about his face is enough to justify my usual "Where are you from?"

I remember the article I read about being a traveler rather than a tourist: the best way to learn a city is by talking to cabbies.

"Where are you from?"

"Russia."

I switch to Russian. "I thought so."

"Why?" he retorts gruffly. Our conversation continues in Russian.

"Your face."

"My face?" he says. "I thought it was my accent."

"You only said one word."

He heads west on Geary.

"Why do you speak Russian?" he asks.

"My father was Russian. I don't use it much anymore. It's rusty."

"No, it's good. You only have a slight accent."

He abruptly changes the subject.

"I had a fare the other day, at rush hour. A tourist couple wanted to go to the wharf. We got stuck in traffic at Kearny and Columbus, behind three busses. The guy became irate, was really rude—he was unbelievable. I decided I wouldn't take his tip; I don't take tips from rude people. But when we got to Pier 39, he threw a twenty-dollar bill at me and ran off. I jumped out, tried to give him the change, but he was gone. It really pissed me off. I don't accept tips from people I don't like."

Scarcely do I have time to acknowledge that story before the driver's onto another.

"I pick up two women, Russian, an older and a younger one. The older one says 'Where are you from?' I say 'Africa.'"

"East Africa?" she asks.

"No, Central Africa."

"Oh. Why are you so light?"

"I lighten my skin. I don't like looking black."

I laugh from my seat in back.

"This older guy gets in one day. He has an accent. Asks me in Russian if I speak Russian. I answer in Russian that I only speak English."

"Oh," he says. "I'm Russian."

"But he's really not, you know."

"What do you mean?" I ask.

The cab driver pauses, glancing at me in the mirror. Then he decides to say it: "He's Jewish."

I remember how shocked I was when my friend

Natasha told me that her mother was Russian, but her father was Jewish. Until then I had never realized that Russian Jews weren't referred to as Russians, even on their identity cards. It was a chilling revelation that distresses me still.

How does the cabbie know, I wonder, that I won't be offended? In fact, I am somewhat; but before I can react, he is onto the rest of the story.

"But he got the better of me," the driver chuckles. "When we arrive, he pays the five dollars on the meter, then hands me a ruble—I mean a dollar—and says, 'That's for your good English.'"

We both laugh.

As we head up Van Ness, the traffic lights are with us. Our wheels keep rolling, as do the driver's stories.

"I pick up another Russian woman. She asks where I'm from, and I say 'Africa.'"

"You speak Russian well, and you have an amazing accent," she says.

"I went to school in Moscow, at Patrice Lumumba University," I tell her.

The cabbie glances at me again to make sure I'm following.

"You know there is such a college in Moscow, full of Africans," he clarifies.

"Then I get another woman, from some fancy house in Pacific Heights. 'Where are you from?' she asks."

I begin to see why cabbies with accents—which is to say, most of them in this city of immigrants—might get tired of being asked their nationality.

"So I say 'Africa,'" he continues.

"Really!" she says.

We pull up to my door, but the driver keeps talking.

"Yes, I'm the son of Nelson Mandela's 108th mistress,"

I tell her.

"If you're the son of Nelson Mandela why do you drive a cab?" she asks.

"It's a social experiment."

I am cracking up, sorry this trip is ending.

"You could have a second career, you know, as a stand cup comic," I comment.

"Oh, no," he replies. "I'm a curmudgeon."

"You're hysterical," I insist, though I know there is much truth to how he sees himself. "But why did you tell me you were Russian instead of African?"

"I don't know. Somehow you seemed genuinely interested."

"Well," I reply, a little taken aback, "it was really nice riding with you. I'm Tania. What's your name?"

"Amil."

"What part of Russia are you from, Amil?"

"I am from Tashkent."

Apparently Amil still thought of geography in Soviet terms.

"My father was a Cossack, from the Don region."

"Really!" he beams. "I am a Tatar!"

It feels like he has just divulged a big secret, one I wish I had more time to explore. The Tatars were the bogeymen of my childhood, the dark-skinned invaders, the Mongol hordes who subjugated the God-loving good guys and wreaked havoc on civilization for more than two hundred years.

"You don't look like a Tatar," I say, looking at his pale, round face. "I always teased my brother about having Tatar blood, but he is dark. He looks like Omar Sharif."

"Your brother is lucky. My brothers are dark, also. I just came out different. I don't usually tell anyone I am Tatar."

I can tell he is launching into another story, but the

doorman is standing outside the van, waiting. We don't have time. As Amil gets out to shake my hand, I quickly add the maximum tip allowed by the cab app, regretting that it is only a few dollars.

"Did you add a tip, Tania?" he asks, saying my name carefully, as if committing it to memory.

"I did. I gave the maximum allowed."

"Great," he replies. "I am honored to take it."

Braving the cold, I rush inside as the taxi drives away, call-light on, ready for the next customer.

Only as I push the elevator button does it occur to me to wonder who he really was, this light-skinned, Russian-speaking storyteller.

16 LAUGHING EYES

Traveling through Central Asia touched me in ways that peeled away years of my life. For the first time since I was young, I was surrounded by people who spoke Russian. People who wanted to know why it was that I, too, spoke the language.

"I am American, but my father was Russian. He left Russia a hundred years ago," I responded. Waiters hovered around me in Bukhara, Uzbekistan, knowing that I would translate any need from a fork to another beer. They saw many French, German, and Italian tourists. But English knocked them flat. They did not see many Americans.

Toward the end of dinner one night, a handsome young lad walked up behind me.

"This is for you," he said gently, handing me a delicate white rose.

It wasn't a real rose. It was a white object that seemed to glow in the open-air caravanserai. A violinist played Mozart, and a singer had just finished a Russian rendition of "Dark Eyes" or "Очи Чёрные."

Just as I had finished explaining to my friends that the

song was about captivating dark eyes, the rose was placed in my hand.

I stumbled through a thank you, and asked, "But why are you giving me this?"

The gracious young man replied, "For your laughing eyes."

I doubt he expected me to leap up and hug him, but how could I resist?

I photographed my rose before going to sleep. I had walked home attentively holding it before me, marveling that someone had turned an ordinary paper napkin into an object that could give me such joy.

17 EVAPORATING WITH THE MISTS

It is five in the morning. I lie on the floor of a large room, empty but for our three bodies. We are protected from the cold by a thick velvet blanket and from a hard tile floor by old chair pads. Roosters crow outside. Pigs grunt below.

My Miao hostess wears traditional dress, chops off chicken heads with practiced grace, and is circumspect as she welcomes strangers foisted on her by surprise. She speaks no English. From her gestures before we went to sleep, we understand that one does one's business "somewhere down there."

There is neither a bathroom in nor an outhouse outside this new three-story home on the village's main road—a cement walkway the width of a car, yet narrower than our bus. At the bottom of the stairs—near the pigs—is a narrow slit, opening onto the steep slope below the house. A hollowed-out log about twenty feet long drops sharply from the slit.

I have my own business to do. But, imagining the pitch-black hillside, I decide I can wait. Our hostess's brother-in-law, the village headman, lives next door. His house, older and lacking the flash of tile floors, nonetheless has an enclosed outhouse—out the door, down a slope, and past the two pigsties. All this, of course, is beyond the few areas lit by long, snaking wires and naked bulbs. I'll have to wait until sunrise to relieve myself there.

The din of roosters grows louder. I hear a door open, followed by footsteps, then watch the lower part of a male in pajamas—lit by the jerking beam of a small flashlight—pass through our space, no doubt heading to the slit at the bottom of the stairs. I do not know how much longer I myself can wait.

I am in Guizhou, a remote province of southern China, with a group of photographers experienced in searching out cultures that retain ancient rituals and celebrations. The Miao is one such culture. Many different tribes of the Miao minority live in the most remote areas of China and still maintain animistic traditions. I wanted to see Miao culture before it disappears in a rapidly changing China.

Nestled between the better-known provinces of Yunnan and Hunan, Guizhou is a land of jagged mountains and deep gullies. Its remote villages are brought closer every day by China's relentless road building—using half the world's cement and adding a thousand kilometers of highway every month. Some villages, however, are still miles up unpaved winding roads, challenging to find and almost inaccessible in the rain.

Anxious to participate in the celebrations, our small group has rambled around for two weeks, prepared to change course the minute Li Qing, our guide and a member of the Black Miao tribe, hears from another headman. Since it is late October and the end of harvest, local festivals are plentiful—the challenge is to reach them in time.

We travel with no fixed itinerary and never know what

to expect: which tribe will be celebrating; whether there will be water buffalo- or bird fighting; whether we will find the road, get rained out, or—as fortunately happened most often—be welcomed to the festivities. The women we see at the festivals wear incredibly complex, colorful embroidered outfits. Led by young pied pipers, they perform circle dances in open fields for hours—or even days—at a time.

This village where we have spent the night is still remote and inaccessible, despite roadbuilding twenty minutes away on a scale that reminds me of the Hoover Dam. My two friends and I are sleeping here because, after seven hours of driving through mist and rain on steep muddy roads, our driver gave up in despair. The village headman offered us shelter.

Loud footsteps now approach the house. There is fierce pounding on the front door. No one but the roosters respond. The pounding stops. Soon I hear the unmistakable sounds of a video game and a child's glee. Voices start below us. A cell phone plays a Chinese ringtone. My friends wake to blaring karaoke-like music next door.

Our quiet voices mingle with the jumble of noises. We discuss the incessant rain, who snored, the rain again, our dreams, and the rain yet again. Soon we decide it is time to use those facilities next door. Doing so, we learn, requires expert aim between a series of logs. The details are better left undescribed.

Yesterday an irresistible trail pulled me away from the last village on a mountain road, through rice terraces and into the forest beyond. Just when I thought I had hit the end of human habitation, a house emerged along the trail. An old woman bent nearly in half and leaning on a walking stick shuffled out. Laughing uproariously, she waved farewell to the neighbor she was gossiping with. We acknowledged each other silently and then set off, our routes converging as we both headed farther down the path.

Half an hour later I still walked slowly next to her, in awe of her determination, undeterred as she seemed to be by her frailty or dependence on the walking stick.

Another village appeared out of the mist. Her neighbors guffawed when they saw us, but she waved them off dismissively.

After leading me through narrow passages, she ushered me into a house. As I walked inside, a chubby baby burst into tears of terror at the sight of my foreign face. A small window lent an ethereal glow to the space. Next to the fire where food was cooked, I was surprised to see a single modernish object: a dirty old Coca-Cola cooler, like the kind from my childhood. A bundle of snarled wires meant the home had electricity, but there was no running water.

The baby's mother ran outside. Soon she returned with a young man carrying a small object. It turned out to be one of the few cell phones in the village. The young man and the woman debated loudly before getting the new device's camera to make me a "prisoner of light," our guide Li's awesome term for photography.

They insisted I sit on the traditional infant-height stool. It put me at eye level with the bent old woman, who had obviously been tiny even before years of stooping and vitamin deficiencies brought her lower still. After the photo session, everyone went about their business as if I weren't even there—sweeping, stirring, chopping. A pot of bones boiled away, steam flowing into the light, and a pig I couldn't see grunted contentedly. I, too, was content.

I managed to turn down an invitation to eat and used gestures to ask how to return to the trail back to civilization. Soon the neighborhood children who materialized, as they always do, were laughing and shouting "bi, bi," to my own "bye, bye," as I retraced my steps and headed back to the nearest road. I hoped my friends weren't wondering where I had disappeared to this time.

"How do you communicate when you share no language?" people constantly ask, when I describe these sorts of interactions. For me, words feel extraneous in such circumstances. The simple joy of being with each other is enough.

At a festival one day I squatted until my feet fell asleep on a grass tussock overlooking a muddy expanse. Water buffalo were expected to fight soon in fierce competition. As I eased my body closer to the sinewy dark-skinned man sitting next to me, catcalls from across the field teased him about his new American girlfriend.

Probably twenty years younger than my sixty-six years, he had already lost most of his teeth. When he smiled, wrinkles etched small canyons in pitted skin. He fumbled with a cigarette and somehow lit it with just one hand, acting as if doing so were the most natural thing in the world.

His right hand held a small red-and-blue-plaid umbrella. It sheltered both of us not from the usual predicted rain, but from a sun that pounded onto skin damp from sweltering humidity. I pretended my position was accidental but remained fixed in the shelter. The wait seemed endless.

The crowds on the surrounding hillside kept growing. An occasional beast broke free and pulled its owner like a toy. Firecrackers were set off. Yet still we waited. As much as, if not more than, the fights themselves, I hoped to see the elaborate dancing that was to precede them.

There were no other white faces in the crowd, but that did not make my photography group the only foreigners. Pink high heels coated in mud gave away Chinese visiting from the city. The local tribeswomen wore beautiful handmade indigo dresses with pink and white embroidered bands over colored tennies; the men, as is often the case in remote corners of the world, looked as though they had shopped at Walmart reject counters. They wore dirty T-shirts and faded tatty pants.

Word got out that the colorful dancing Miao girls refused to dance—the field was too muddy! When I spied my group leaving, I bowed to my swain and thanked him with a "*shie, shie.*" He grinned in acknowledgment of our brief relationship. As his friends whistled, I shook his hand in parting.

Soon I was on a longboat crossing the river back to the bus, heading to another village, another rumored harvest festival.

As the bus drove along a muddy road, I thought about contrasts. The past dissolves slowly in much of the world. In China it is vaporizing.

We started this trip in Guiyang—the capital of Guizhou province—a city of four million with a giant underground

Walmart anchoring its city center. In the hustle and bustle above the store, a woman painted beautiful calligraphy on the sidewalk. She used a giant brush that looked like a mop but worked like magic. This new kind of disappearing art, called *dishu*, is apparently popular in cities all over China.

A few years ago, Guiyang was a remote provincial town of several hundred thousand, some days by truck or train from Guilin, in a neighboring province. Three years ago an eight-lane freeway was completed between them; this year a high-speed train. At the end of my stay, it took me two hours to make the journey on a smooth train that traveled at over 250 kilometers an hour.

I travel constantly to remote parts of the world. Every time I take a picture of a woman in a bright sari building a road or a nearly naked Samburu herding a goat, I wonder if it's my last time to do so. But the past lingers in those places, even as increased affluence ushers in the present.

In China the past is eviscerated through development. Thousands of miles of highway are completed annually. Towns of a hundred thousand apartments are launched seemingly overnight. In village after village, almost every building is being reconstructed or newly built. Almost every building! The government gives people fifty percent of the new home's value and loans them the rest to encourage progress. A middle class is being created en masse out of mountain hinterlands.

After the canceled dance performance, we drove endlessly in the rain, looking for a village that only a year ago could be reached on small, rarely used dirt roads. Eventually we reached a dead-end, one more road under construction. In front of us lay dirt and fields and nothingness. Next to us was a colorful school. We turned around.

Almost instantly we found ourselves on a paved four-lane road lined by huge high-rises. A woman carrying a giant pile of greens chased her goats across the street. She disappeared down stairs leading to a completed but seemingly empty housing tower fifteen stories high. Red fluorescent writing flashed across the entry of a large building across the way—perhaps a hotel—not yet completed. This mini-city was just two blocks long and one block wide. The other end was yet another mud road and more nothingness.

The young are moving in droves to these instant cities, leaving elders to watch their remote villages empty out. Rice terraces are going wild as people become too old to work them and rice too cheap to be worth the effort. Other terraces are being replaced with passion fruit orchards—this year's hot commodity—planted by large farm cooperatives. Some villages are being rebuilt as tourist attractions—complete with Disneyland-type open-air buses, entry fees, and regularly scheduled ceremonial dances.

Running into his sister at a large multi-tribe harvest festival, our guide, Li, learns that his village is marked for a new road by next year.

"They aren't ready yet," he bemoans. "We need a few more years."

"But you live in the city. How often do you visit?"

"Rarely. I hardly have the time. My parents are both dead, and my sister takes care of my property. But I will go back."

This Miao man is in his early forties. He has been in the

city since college and has married a woman of the Dong tribe, something that would have been unimaginable back in his village. He tells me he wants to move back when he is "older" because of friends and family, and because "people take care of each other" in the village.

"But does your wife want to go back?" I ask.

He looks at me as if surprised by the question; he hasn't really considered it.

"Well, no," he finally answers. "She likes running water, the flushing toilet, the convenience of the shopping, the good school for the kids."

"Are there any other Dong people in your village?"

"Not really." He pauses. "No. It is a Miao village."

"Wouldn't that be hard for her?"

"Yes…"

I visualize the life he would have had in that village in an era in which parents arranged marriages within the tribe, women moved in with their in-laws, and oldest sons inherited homes enlarged at great sacrifice by their parents. It was a life that today would make no sense for him, even if his village weren't about to be bulldozed beyond recognition.

I suspect he will never move back to that village; it may well disappear long before he stops working. His children will have little connection to it, especially with no living grandparents. He still harbors a romantic notion of the past he fled but, like the impermanent calligraphy on the cement of Guiyang, his primitive homeland is evaporating like water on a hot sidewalk.

High on an isolated mountaintop, a Miao village shaman declared the day auspicious for a harvest festival. Li heard about it from the second cousin of his sister's mother-in-law. He ensured we got there in time for the final preparations.

Now we were surrounded by colorful young women. But Li, who had participated in remote Miao tribal celebrations all his life, was enthusing about a group of gnarly old men playing ancient bamboo mouth organs called *lushengs*. The lusheng, often more than six feet long, is considered a means of communicating with the spirit world, its music honoring the deceased. It is key to these ceremonies. Whiny and wheezy, the instruments were far from the sophisticated specimens whose more dulcet tones flow pleasingly to Western ears. No, this music would not make my playlist.

In other villages and at celebrations by several different tribes, including the famous Long Horn Miao and the Short Skirt Miao, we had heard never-ending performances of a wide variety of lushengs—mostly by young men of seemingly inexhaustible energy. I had learned that the dances helped young women choose husbands. And I understood why the welcome we received from a group of creaky old men was unique, for they normally ceded the festivities to the young and bold.

At the end of the trip, a friend and I explored the countryside around Guilin, a land of mystical karst mountains and rice terraces whose haunting beauty—clear, reflecting rivers and hobbit-hiding landscapes—has filled my dreams for years.

The weather, however, didn't cooperate. By the last day of our time in the countryside, unexpected deluges had flooded rivers and emptied rural pathways. I was scheduled to fly out of Guilin the next morning, but more downpours made getting back to the city problematic. I didn't make it until late at night, stuck in traffic and unable to see much through the banging windshield wipers. After my early wake-up call the next morning, I learned that my plane was delayed eight hours.

I opened my eyes a while later to a respite from the rain. Shorty after, I stepped out of my elegant hotel to discover a broad river swollen with stormwater. On the wide, paved riverbank about a hundred people danced synchronized steps to ballroom music blaring from a boom box. Elsewhere, I saw walkers overflowing onto busy streets. Boats plied the water, which had flooded a pathway below. The noise of the traffic—competing with the rushing water and music—pushed me along, past shopping streets, more hotels, high-rises, and office blocks.

My wandering eventually took me away from the busy city streets. Soon I was following curving cobblestone paths along seemingly endless waterways. Carved white railings lined narrow bridges; pavilions and temples filled small islands. Local tourists posed for pictures. Some wore garish tribal costumes they had rented; others five-inch heels complementing red-streaked hair and skin-tight pants.

A choir practiced in an alcove, sword-ballet dancers found another. Card-playing and mah-jongg filled various nooks. A dumpy middle-aged fisherwoman cleaned two ugly carp, while nearby a group of men threw lines with no luck.

I couldn't stop walking toward the karst hills visible through distant mists, although I knew I risked getting lost. The river had already split and then split again. I started worrying about the time.

But then I heard an eerily familiar music. I followed it,

finding my way to a narrow café along the riverbank. Inside, six old-timers—local musicians pausing for a cigarette break—offered me a smoke and a seat. I chose a stool—relieved that my denial of the cigarette, a less than courteous response in such circumstances, hadn't caused offense—and relaxed.

One of the men began serenading me with a musical pipe. His neighbor joined in, followed by a woman playing a small xylophone-like instrument. Soon my whole personal chamber orchestra was playing, grinning broadly at me.

The lead singer excitedly pointed at the piece they had selected, insisting that I read markings that were—of course—Chinese to me. I photographed the page with my iPhone and emailed it to my Chinese-speaking neighbor, Julie. From seven thousand miles away she responded almost immediately, explaining that the Chinese characters:

欢迎你到桂林来

meant I was being warmly welcomed to the green mountains of Guilin.

I showed my new friends the reply. We all beamed, as if proud to have bridged the language divide. They played more music as I sat by, slowing into the moment.

Some shaman on my travels must have spoken some magic words, the spirit world inducing these elders to play this music I now cherished. I reflected back to the remote villages, talking to people I couldn't understand and listening to the incomprehensible tones. Now I didn't want to leave; I wanted to stay, to sink deeper into an experience that had created coherence out of cacophony—but I had a plane to catch.

The group paused, and the lead singer hugged me for a photo. Both of us were inexplicably near tears. I thanked the group for my personal concert and turned to go. My new friends followed me outside, waving goodbye and offering up some final plaintive chords.

I captured those precious tones for the A-list on my playlist.

18 INTO A DISAPPEARING DEEP

A beautifully muscled body soars to the apex of a majestic leap, painting a perfect arc over my head. Clouds billow in the late-afternoon sun and light glints on the sea. The diver's long spear touches the water. A moment later he's gone. Only an empty dugout canoe bobs in the water next to me. Standing in a small dinghy, I balance my weight to absorb the rocking and wait for the free-diving Moken fisherman to reappear.

My travel group had raised anchor at four in the morning, heading for the village of Ma Kyone Galet, on a tiny spit of land off the southern coast of Myanmar. Somewhere along the way, near a mangrove swamp, an encounter awaited with the sea nomads known as Moken and their traditional *kabangs*, or longboats.

Or so we thought.

The Moken evaded us as we sailed across constantly changing seas.

Moken by nature had been wayfarers, nomads, roamers who shifted their homes when the environment forced a change. The very name "Moken" means "drowned in the sea" in their language, and it seems the original people were driven from land centuries ago by the Mon, a famed tribe of artists and architects. On the edges of the Mon culture were people unable to continue fighting for their territory and too restless to adapt—people who escaped to uninhabited islands and waterways.

For thousands of years, the Moken wandered the Andaman Sea, among islands that lie off the coast of today's Myanmar and Thailand. They had kabangs with woven palm-frond covers big enough to sleep and cook under, and a way of deftly leaping from the bow, spear first, into deep waters, reemerging with a fish for the next meal.

The Moken didn't teach their children how to dive, how

to see underwater, or how to hold their breath for longer than might seem possible to outsiders. They passed their knowledge on through instinct.

When the tsunami of 2004 hit their homeland, the Moken's instincts spurred them to action. They knew that waters departing from the shores meant something powerful was coming. They ran to the hills. Many survived.

The tsunami, however, ruined boats and structures. It sped up the disintegration of the Moken's way of life. Large motorized fishing boats then came from far away to these rich waters, ignoring laws and fishing indiscriminately, robbing more Moken of their livelihoods. By the time of my visit, the last authentic nomadic kabang in the region had been abandoned some ten years ago.

Searching for these nomads of the waters, my group finally understood that we would not find them at sea. The Moken were hidden in plain sight.

On land.

By late afternoon we approached Ma Kyone Galet, originally planned as a model village at the edge of a natural park, a way to help the Moken adjust to losing the freedom of the seas. But they struggled to survive, and tourists, like the nomads, continued to be elusive in Myanmar. Eventually the village became a mixed community of a few hundred people—as big a metropolis as can be found in the area. Today over half the residents are Burmese. The two cultures are weaving together, although the Moken still largely live in homes built on stilts over the water, tying their boats to their houses and merging the worlds of sea and land.

The first thing we saw as we approached the village were dugout canoes with tiny children rowing toward us. It was pouring rain, but they were determined in their onslaught. We were charmed. But the children were mostly after the instant noodles and canned sodas the crew had brought for them.

The tide was far out as I jumped into the broad shallows of a rock-strewn shore. Footing was tenuous because hidden currents flowed between the shore and the nearby mangrove swamps, but the scene proved irresistible. My feet sank in the shifting sands, my waterproof sneakers effectively retained the water that flooded in, and my knees found the sharp hidden rocks as I knelt for perspective for my photos.

Beached longboats and dugout canoes lay scattered around me, their shapes reflected in the wet sands. Dramatic clouds covered the sky, and smoke filled the air. Some of the boats were deeply entrenched, perhaps permanently. Their wood had no need for artful antiquing;

long contact with saltwater guaranteed a rustic patina. Their very survival required constant maintenance.

Many of the boats were elevated on rocks or boards under which palm-frond fires were lit. Men and women folded themselves into ampersand shapes around the fires, aiming plumes of smoke at the bottoms and sides of the boats. Smells of old oil and something gummy filled the air. I learned later that the process kills moths, cleans algae, and seals oil into the wood, beautifying it as a side effect.

The scene kept evolving as I shifted perspective. To one side, a narrow inlet, a few palm trees, intriguing reflections, a Buddhist pagoda backing up to forest. The other way, a collage of boats stretched to houses on stilts. The sky played a continuously changing counterpoint to this symphony of impressions. The swirls of fanned smoke kept it all from settling into simple reality.

The workers laughed as I leaped around, splashing and pointing my camera at them. Eventually, when the tide started turning, I headed to the homes.

Crude huts of bamboo, tin, and tarps with rickety decks perched in the air. Fish hung from the eaves, drying. A woman pulled snails out of the sand under her home. Another one filleted fresh flatfish. A young man soaped his body, grinning as he spied me. An old woman stepped from her home into my scene, both of us surprised by our meeting.

I wandered to the Buddhist temple on the Burmese side of town and watched a ceremony that involved taking a golden figure out on a boat. The ceremony was sparsely attended. Many more people gathered to watch the cockfight that followed after the golden god departed.

I heard laughter, and peered into a dark repair shack to see six glowing eyes gazing at me. Three young men covered in grease and wearing dirty Western hand-me-downs squatted as they worked on an old motor from one of the longtail boats. They smiled as I caught their eyes, then returned to their work.

I dropped back to the sand at the water's edge. There I stumbled onto a group of women sitting on the ground, playing cards and joyously betting and shouting, surrounded by little children. Older children hauled in pails of water from the town pumps, then jumped about in the rising waters of the sea. Monks headed back to the temple. Delicate nets were being repaired everywhere I turned.

The rain cleared. My group headed back on the water, entering the realm of the Burmese—those with motorized boats rather than the handmade artifacts of an ancient way of life. We saw a small fleet of longtail motorboats resting in a secluded inlet nearby, and we rowed out to visit them. They were waiting for the large ships to come purchase their catch and restock their ice. We were searching for fish for our dinner. The first boat we met had a handful of foot-long fish in their hold, but we wanted a few more. A fisherman on the next ship pulled out a few beautiful flatfish, slightly shorter but wider. I leaned precariously over the hold to see more clearly, and suddenly understood why the fishing nets were so fine. Stashed on ice were plastic crates of tiny, fragile squid. They were sorted by size—the largest no bigger than a finger. The local village had a couple of handfuls of large squid next to an old green scale, but these little delicacies were headed for the choicest markets of China or Japan.

As evening neared, the fleet grew exponentially. Our guide had been here many times but was shocked at the number of boats in the cove. At night, their strong lights seduced the fish into their nets. The beautiful sea is being fished out. The traditional fishing of the Moken has no chance against this new armada.

As we headed back to our ship, a dugout canoe with a young man at the oars approached.

"Would you like to see him dive?"

We certainly would.

He arcs into that water, at one with the sea and the clouds.

I see him swimming in the deep, holding his breath, chasing the elusive fish, his eyes bright with magical underwater vision. I see him return with his catch to his family in their palm-frond covered boat, floating in an empty sea. I see his ancestors...

His sudden splash jerks me back to the present.

Those bright eyes are now covered with a modern mask—a gift from a previous tourist. He is not going to bring his dinner with him when he comes back up for air. It's a performance. It's just for us. But as I watch the skill, grace, and elegance of this young man's dance with the sea, the story of the Moken takes on a heartbreaking perspective.

He dove into a familiar deep.

Where, I wonder, as I gaze at those shifting seas, will he emerge?

19 A PRECIOUS GIFT

I was sharing the wooden floor of a primitive home with a group of chattering women when one of them jumped up, called out something incomprehensible, and scrambled down the rough stairs, pointing at me. I started to follow but was gently held back by hands tapping my knees. Just a moment earlier I had felt so close to that woman that her departure felt like abandonment.

Why was she leaving me? Was I the only one who had felt the connection?

On reaching the muddy ground below us, the tiny, gray-haired lady—head wrapped in a handwoven scarf, her proud figure as straight as a young woman's—slipped her feet into old flip-flops and danced through rain puddles out of the enclosure. She ran along the bank of the river in a direction I had not explored. Words of explanation swirled around me, but I understood none of them. All I could do was sip my tea, nod my head, and force a smile.

It was late 2016, and I was traveling in a remote part of Myanmar, along the upper reaches of the Chindwin River. I had visited the country several times, but we were now traveling further north than had been possible previously, in distant areas that were opening up as the country's political situation improved.

Just five years earlier, the military junta had been in firm control and opposition leader Aung San Suu Kyi had been under house arrest. Minorities were at war throughout the northern part of the country. Yangon was a poor but bustling city with many old colonial buildings and rare signs of the twenty-first century. There were less than 250,000 private cars in a country with a population far greater than California's. As recently as the last day of 2012, I had used the very first ATM in Myanmar.

Now Aung San Suu Kyi was the elected head of government and had just visited the United Nations; President Obama had eliminated trade sanctions against Myanmar; most tribal wars in the north had at least temporarily ceased. Yangon was a city suffering total traffic gridlock, and construction of massive towers had eliminated much of the colonial feel. Street vendors who once sold nail clippers and hairpins now competed for business with cheap smart phones and gaudy covers. SIM cards for $1.50 had replaced ones that had cost $1,500.

After only a brief time in the crowded city, we had ventured into areas little touched by commercial development. Here villagers were still hoping for electricity and running water, although young people were climbing to the high points—where golden pagodas stood—not only to pray, but to find cell reception. A relative freedom had permeated even to them, and pictures of Aung San Suu Kyi proudly hung on the walls of their simple homes, constructed as they had been for centuries.

I wanted to experience this countryside before commercialism expanded further. We traveled where no tourists had gone, driving for five hours through pounding rain along steep mudslides and increasingly narrow, unpaved roads to a remote village. There we would help the villagers learn how to greet and house visitors, generating funds that could help bring them solar-powered energy.

A longhouse had been constructed just for us. A pig was eviscerated and roasted in our honor; the women sang and danced for hours; the men played on a giant drum fashioned from a hollowed tree surely a hundred years old.

The next day we visited the local children in their one-room schoolhouse. We watched rice being pounded and large pails of water being carried by women and girls who seemed much too small to support the weight. It felt as though we had slipped into a previous century.

Leaving the village behind a few days later, we continued our exploration by boat.

One morning we stopped at a riverside settlement of about a hundred houses. The community stretched along the shore near the town of Khamti, some five hundred miles north of Mandalay. I left our boat and wandered off alone.

I walked past an open-fronted general store. A pharmacist sorted pills while, on the floor, a dog slept and a child yawned. A young girl snipped heads off tiny fish in her front yard. A woman effortlessly balanced two buckets of water and her child, while pausing to smile at me. A water buffalo stared suspiciously from the side of the road, one that showed no tire tracks.

In a field I passed shortly after, a mechanical contraption had replaced the usual wooden plow pulled by water buffalo or oxen. A device that would have been at home in America back when Ford was first experimenting with cars, it looked like it had given up the ghost halfway through the field, even though the plot was small enough to be plowed by hand. A large yellow gas container, old and dirty, sat nearby. It all had the sad air of a failed experiment.

As I passed a large Buddhist pagoda and temple near the center of the village, a small crowd formed as women departed the temple grounds. I paused to watch.

One of the last to exit was a delicate lady wrapped in harvest-colored scarves, whose smile formed deeply creased wrinkles testifying to over eighty years of life. She held a bunch of flowers and graciously posed for a photo, removing her woven, wide-brimmed hat before continuing on. Another woman, sharing the predominant erect and slender figure of the locals, stood next to me. We observed the scene and, eventually, each other.

That was how it started—our friendship.

When I reached to clasp her hand in greeting, she held

mine in silent welcome. She didn't let go. Soon we were walking. I'm not sure what prompted her to lead me down that riverfront dirt road, but we strolled together, smiling at the questioning glances of her neighbors. Near the end of the village, she turned and led me into a neatly tended yard with a few women and children.

It was the simplest of settings, but there was a subtle sophistication here. Geometrically defined homesteads were delineated with unobtrusive stick fencing. Gardens were tended and graced with decorative flowers. Houses were raised on poles to protect from high rainy-season river levels and were built of teak or other local wood. Each lot had a designated entry and adequate room for animal enclosures away from the house. The homes had palm-frond roofs, and many had a large open wall to the south. They were single-room dwellings with no electricity or running water, with wood fires for cooking, but large enough so that dark corners afforded some privacy.

The houses ran along the river. Those in the center were fronted with shops, with fields behind them. This village had avoided the chaos of others we had seen, where the discovery of gold had led to large-scale mining and devastated landscapes, which were left deserted after the veins were depleted. But the fact that there was no wealth here to exploit also meant there was nothing to help economic development. There were no fancy luxuries or tourist goods in the small shops. There were few alternatives to leaving the village for schooling and work.

As my walking partner and I approached her home, raised off the ground and open to the elements, surprise on faces gave way to welcome. I removed my soggy trail runners and climbed to join a casual group having tea. Soon I was drinking the delicious home-dried green tea I have loved since discovering it on my first trip to this country years ago. It has a delicate flavor and lacks the after-bite I usually associate with green tea. I have tasted the best teas in the gardens of Assam and the teashops of San Francisco, but nothing has compared to sharing this home brew in the villages of Myanmar. I savored that first sip and was rewarded with many refills.

Although conversations swirled around me, my friend and I had yet to exchange a single word. Here on the Chindwin we were far beyond the reach of Burmese, and even our translator—had he been anywhere near—would have struggled to help me. Over a hundred different languages are spoken in Myanmar, belonging to five major language families. That tiny woman and I, for sure, had no shared language. We connected without one.

I eventually got a young girl to take pictures of us. I tried to pose sitting on my knees as they all did, but the hard, uneven wood surface undermined my attempts. My knees could almost bear it, but the tops of my feet screamed in agony. Watching the women sit there, unperturbed by any discomfort, helped me understand their excellent posture. Their shoulders were relaxed and their backs easily straight, their feet tucked unobtrusively, as if they were geishas in a Kyoto teahouse rather than peasant farmwives. Their innate elegance of bearing was remarkable.

When she finished her tea, my friend reached for a tray of green betel leaves. I caught her eye for approval before I started recording a video. I'm still waiting for a translation of the amused chatter that accompanied the wrapping of her chaw and its quick insertion into her mouth, but I know they all enjoyed my fascination. Normally, betel chewing is something done a bit surreptitiously, when strangers aren't observing. There are ongoing government attempts to educate people against chewing betel—as addictive as cigarettes—but her generation was beyond that, their teeth already destroyed with the characteristic red rot that keeps their smiles hidden. By agreeing to let me film her, my friend showed me I was no longer a stranger.

Instead, she and I bonded as we watched the video again and again, giggling like schoolgirls while everyone else angled in for a look.

And then my friend suddenly jumped up and ran away.

Now that she was gone, I started wondering how to extricate myself from this household that, just minutes ago, had seemed like a haven.

My friend ran back into the yard, climbed up to our perch, and settled next to me. In her hand was a small bracelet of golden-brown beads of amber. She reached for my arm and solemnly put the warm-toned bracelet on my wrist, securing the adjustable silk band and grinning at its fit. My tiny wrist was the perfect size for her offering. I stared at it and at her, then hugged her in gratitude, tearing up in my surprise at this unexpected gift.

It was the most unlikely of events. A passing stranger who lived in the wealthiest country in the world randomly encountered a woman living in the simplest of circumstances in one of the poorest countries of the world. The latter woman's material possessions probably amounted to almost nothing; the stranger might have carried assets equal to the village woman's total net worth in her carry-on luggage. The two women were not likely to ever see each other again.

I was the woman who had everything. She was the one who, by any economic measure, had nothing. Yet it was she who brought me a gift.

And not just any gift: a bracelet of amber. A product almost one hundred million years old, far older than the better-known Baltic amber. Beads her son-in-law must have dug out of a deep hole in the ground; ones her daughter polished while sitting in that same lovely kneeling position as the women did now, in much cruder circumstances and with an old metal wheel grinding noisily.

Some years ago, when I started on my path of travel and exploration, writing, and photography, my most important discovery was that I should simply say "Yes!" to opportunity. Accepting something without the possibility of giving anything in return, however, isn't always comfortable. It's much easier to give than to receive. But, again, that's not always possible.

I had nothing but my affection to give in return.

Somehow I knew that was enough, all my friend wanted or would accept. To offer anything more would have been an insult.

I joyously accepted her gift, thanked her in all the wrong languages, and gave her another big hug.

We walked hand in hand back through the town, met some family members, and sat with her grandson at the village gate. When the time eventually came to say goodbye, I went to find our guide.

Our acquaintance lasted only a short time, but I was able to learn that my new friend's name was Daw Htay Han. My guide explained that she shared my age of sixty-seven years, her daughter and son-in-law lived and worked in an amber mine, and her grandson was one of four novices living in the Buddhist temple.

Today I also know that her village is called Malin, a place I can pinpoint to within thirty feet on a map by using the geotagging information on my photographs. I also know that there are no entries about the village on the Internet, no photos, no awareness. It is several days journey by river south from the most likely location of the even more remote amber mines where her daughter works, and two days journey upriver from Homalin, the last town with any identifiable Internet presence—full of news of another overcrowded ferryboat disaster just days before our arrival. It seemed little else there was newsworthy.

My photos show that, in addition to our age, physically Daw Htay and I had more in common than not. We were of similar height and weight. Our eyes were equally dark, and our hair was turning gray—hers faster than mine. Her skin was darker and her nose flatter, and she kept her lips close to hide her ruined teeth, while my smile boasted the aligned white caps that cover my original crooked teeth. Our eyes were both similarly wrinkled, however, and twinkled with our mutual affection.

I don't know many other specifics of Daw Htay's life. I do know she is a woman as comfortable in her own skin as

I have learned to be in mine; one who called me sister and beamed when introducing me to her grandson. We didn't need words; we had a common language. Words might have gotten in the way of a mutual understanding that went deeper, friendship and a memory that would carry across thousands of miles.

At home in San Francisco, I finger the stones of my bracelet as if they were worry beads and think about Daw Htay's daughter polishing each one by hand. They turn warm and their pleasing pearly finish takes me back...

20 CUBA IN COLOR

Join me on the lively plaza in the heart of Camagüey, Cuba.

I am seated in a restaurant, sipping an after-dinner drink. I've tabled my camera, and I'm taking in the whole scene.

Turn your head just a bit. Look.

Old streetlamps send a warm glow onto dark skin. Sculpted bodies parade with an ease that makes San Francisco seem puritan in contrast.

Then she appears. Bold red pants cup her impossibly curved buttocks. Endless legs lead down into tall heels that somehow click rather than clunk. Dancing hips pull up, up, and up through the swaying movements of generous breasts to the brief gleam of a dark, smiling face. A swish of long hair flashes as she disappears into the crowd. All eyes follow in the hope of one more glimpse.

It could be a dimly lit square from an old impressionist painting. But that overdressed era lacked the excitement of a key ingredient: a woman of Cuba. And that ingredient, this particular Cuban woman, reached deep into my psyche. She was an agent of irresistible seduction to this land of contrasts. She was why I left my heart in this town that first captured my imagination as I wandered its early-morning-empty cobblestones, then seduced me with its sultry warmth and irrepressible creativity.

Camagüey is pronounced *come-away*—yes, as in "come away with me." It calls to me still to come away to its gentle beauty, its mazed streets, its beautiful women, its art.

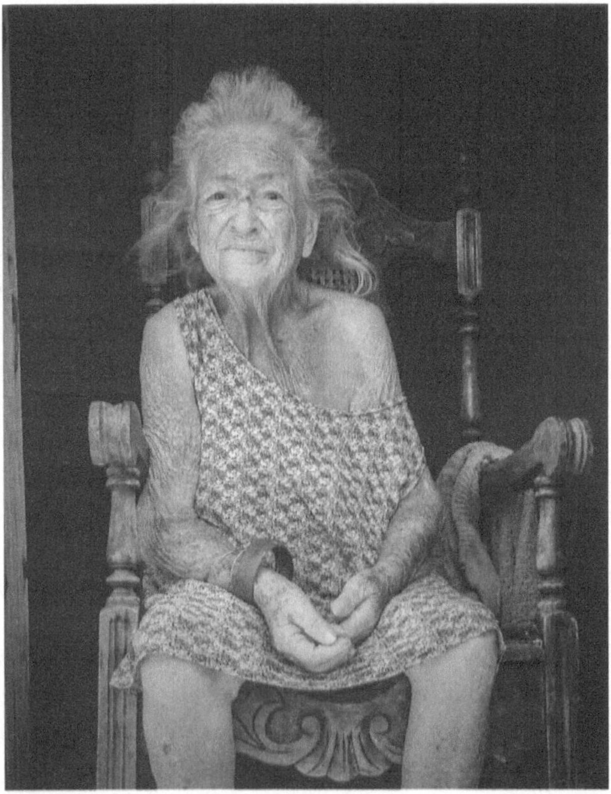

My own art takes a significant leap forward in those streets.

I walk past an ancient doorway. A gaunt, timeworn woman gazes at me, at first with nervous tension, a moment later relaxed. I see her curiosity, her thinning skin, the details of the darkness she sits in, the knitting on the shawl over the seat of an old carved wooden chair. She doesn't mind that I take her photograph.

The lack of a giant camera has prevented intimidation, the push-button ease of the camera on my phone has helped me capture the spirit I see and feel. I am able to focus on her soul, rather than managing sophisticated technology.

I finally understand: my iPhone is the only camera I need.

The revelation starts me on a path that still gives me great joy.

"Camagüey, quaintest and least known of Cuban cities, is a storehouse of delight to the casual visitor and a source of undying joy to the man behind the camera, for in Camagüey the sixteenth century clasps hands with the twentieth, across streets so narrow that each carriage driver should possess a pilot's license to navigate them in safety."

Written in 1905 by Elisa Armstrong Bengough, this description could be adapted to my own visit by simply replacing the man with a woman and the twentieth century with the twenty-first.

The streets might be a bit wider, the buildings more decrepit, but a wide plaza now links two neighborhoods, with seating, shops, and cafés sprouting along its length. Plenty of alleys invite slow exploration.

In the early morning, as most people sleep, the street sweepers mingle with a few cats. Years of habit see me up and about. The glint of well-worn cobblestones pulls me along to a bread hawker setting up his cart. I breathe in the aroma of fresh loaves and anticipate his seductive wake-up calls.

The street hawkers' carts speak to the artistic nature of this town. The decrepit three-wheeled wooden vehicles are pushed along streets where few cars interfere with their passage. These carts are artfully decorated, with garlic strands hanging just so and onions sorted by size and color.

At an outdoor market, a young man whose recycled T-shirt says "Wonderful and funny" smiles and waves at me with the string of onions he is tying. A dank storeroom hides a man surrounded by bright-green bananas whose smile glows in the dark, demanding to be memorialized.

A pig's head might not be everyone's idea of welcoming, but one dangles by its ear with an irresistible grin in front of a tiny comestibles stand called *La Sin Rival*—the Without Equal—to advertise fresh pork. Most cuts of meat are about a dollar a pound, but the head is only a quarter. The inside of the stand is decorated meticulously. The owner spends hours making sure every vegetable is positioned just so.

The pulse of life is somehow gentler here than in other parts of Cuba, as if the very environment were telling you to slow down, look around, enjoy. Pedicabs burst with colorful, bold and unique designs. People sell flowers on the street—often plastic, but beautiful nonetheless. Art is scattered widely. And not just the pervasive, institutionalized revolutionary statues that grace every central square throughout this land.

In one square the sculptress Martha Jiménez has positioned bronze women exhibiting rolls of fat that might embarrass, but are instead flaunted, as they are by people all around me. I envision her unique sculpted fountain in my yard, featuring a laughing, well-endowed, nearly naked woman—bent in a manner that would have my thighs screaming—her healthy stream of urine watering what lies beneath. Almost alive, she gazes at me with a *why are you staring at me?* gleam in her eyes.

Another artist exhibits faces pressed onto thin leather, fading into a background of tobacco leaf. Elsewhere, along a nondescript street, an improbable set of giant faces has been created by chipping white stucco off the walls of a ruined building. My only clue to the artist is the name "Alexander" written across the stucco. The exposed bricks provide dimensionality, and the figures look as though they are emerging from the wall. It is brilliant—and ephemeral. I have since learned that those walls have been torn down.

I walk past four little girls sitting in a windowsill the width of two women's bottoms. As I focus on the scene, they adopt seductive poses that were surely learned from their older sisters.

Nearby, a much older woman pulls me into her home to show me pictures of her granddaughters, displayed on an old wall whose texture I would pay dearly to replicate in my own bedroom. Around eighty, she still wears clothing more revealing than anything I own, bearing weathered skin and wrapping large, sagging breasts that surely comforted more than just her infants.

I recently returned to Cuba to spend a week in Havana. My own country is struggling with leadership that feels repressive and a growing awareness that women are not getting an even chance. I was more conscious than ever how difficult the path of life was for the women here in Cuba.

The main squares in Cuban cities are anchored with statues of its revolutionary leaders. "Never forget" might as well be plastered everywhere. And how *could* anyone forget? It seems to me that these famous heroes—these men—displayed in the squares of every town brought a revolution that shattered but has yet to reach the stage of rebuilding. One that talked of equality for women but left behind mostly decrepit buildings and dead men frozen in bronze. One that empowered the few and impoverished the rest. The men set off a revolution that blazed more fiercely than fireworks but fizzled into a state that would lead a less resilient people into despair.

Yet the women of Cuba walk tall and proud. Once more I am torn between the joys of walking through this world that hasn't evolved much in sixty years and my anger at the men in power who help keep it that way.

My guide on the current trip is a young woman named Yoli. I am amazed to discover she lives in Camagüey.

As befits a sophisticated tour leader, Yoli is more demurely attired than how I remember the women in Camagüey. But as I stare at her gorgeous face, her lovely figure, I wonder if she might not have been one of those beautiful women I observed walking through the squares of that lovely town.

Yoli could well have been the one who inspired my rapture, for she is beautiful in body, soul, and spirit. No request is too challenging, whether for an interview with a baseball team or a visit to a ritual burning of an idol. Early in the morning or late at night, her smile glows, as she shares her knowledge with overprivileged strangers who try to dig deeper into her psyche and that of her homeland.

Yoli could leave Cuba to find a better life in America; her independent spirit would thrive in our country. But she wants to stay. She wants to help her homeland move into the future. I don't know if I could love a land enough to make that kind of sacrifice. My own life in the United States has allowed a success unimaginable in Cuba. But my background as an immigrant from a communist country—an immigrant who left not long before Yoli's country fought its way through its own revolution—leaves me grateful I didn't have to choose.

Yoli's country should be grateful for her determination to stay and make a difference. Cuba should recognize her and all the women that nourish their land, women who impressed me with their resilience and their strength, yet disturbed me with their political invisibility.

My thoughts return to that long-ago night in Camagüey's square. To sitting and drinking mojitos. To watching passersby. To the procession of sexy women whose memory has coaxed me into walking taller and jutting my own ample bosom out a little more; into swaying my butt a bit, as perhaps I should have those many years ago when I was their age.

Again she appears before me. She is a unique beauty; she is all the women I have seen and heard in Cuba.

Hers is the sculpture that, if placed in town squares, would energize a new era better than any dead revolutionary hero. Hers is the body and heart that will expand and nurture Cuba's next generation. Hers will be the raucous laughter—when she is eighty—that will welcome strangers as she shares photos of her youth and her grandchildren.

She is Cuba.

21 KILO KARINGA

Before me, in a remote village of the Zemba tribe in northern Namibia, stood three generations of women: twenty-six-year-old Kilo, her mother, and her Grandmother Muponge, the second wife of the village chief.

"My mother needs you to bring this picture back to her when you return," said Kilo, quietly translating an urgent message and pointing at the two women.

I watched as Kilo's mother held Grandmother Muponge—her own mother—in a close embrace, black skins gleaming in the early evening light. As I raised my camera, Kilo's mother reached lovingly for the naked, long-spent breast that suckled her in infancy. She cupped her hand around it firmly, holding the most precious gift of her life. Her other arm enfolded the tiny old woman, their faces touching. Their eyes were fixed on but reached through me. Their gazes sent a deeply personal message into the future, to those who will follow, to lives beyond their imagination. Through tears that left traces on my dust-coated face, I focused, then dropped my camera after a single click. For me, like a singular, surreal icon, as holy as any I have seen, this image expressed life's most elemental love. The moment touched deep within me, my mind relegating it to a space alongside my own dear mother, whose breast I last touched well over sixty years ago, an infant myself.

The sun set on the group of huts, mud, dung, and thatch. Families moved toward the squash and porridge bubbling in black pots on campfires. I promised to return in the morning. Kilo pointed to her mother's form walking toward the fields. I was reminded she desperately needed a blanket. In the time we had shared, Kilo never asked one thing for herself, although she alone among the villagers had the language faculties and bond with me that would have made it easy to do so.

I wrote these notes while on a photographic expedition deep in a tribal area of Namibia with a friend. She explores so openheartedly that suspicious strangers relax before her lens. When returning to an area, she always brings printed images of the people living there. She carried over five hundred of them on this trip alone.

In some ways this remote world is fixed in an ancient past; in others it is changing fast. Solar-charged cell phones, for example, appear in the most unlikely of spots. But printed photographs—familiar faces memorialized on paper—are still almost unheard of—and treasured. Recipients' eyes light up, inhibitions dissolve into joy, and I, lucky to be a part, am welcomed and invited into lives that would otherwise be inaccessible to me.

The particular tribe my friend hoped to revisit had moved on. A terrible drought had settled over this entire desert area, and the tribe could no longer sustain their lives here. We heard they had shifted north, into the foothills, where their cattle could feed on nourishing grasses.

A young man herding goats mentioned the tribe might have relatives in a nearby village. It was straight north across the desert, he told us.

Our overland vehicle wove around shrubs, across gullies, and through deep sand, following indistinct tracks made by feet and hooves. Ours were the only wheels to leave an unmistakable mark on the trajectory.

Somehow our guide's instincts led us to a set of huts enclosed by the usual woven-twig fences. None of the tribespeople moved to greet us; they just stared in expectant silence. Moving gently, as if approaching a shying animal, our guide entered and talked to the watchful inhabitants. Eventually he showed them some photos. They recognized a woman, a distant relation they hadn't seen for some time. Faces relaxed. The village headman was found. We were invited in.

A young woman wandered over, watching the scene calmly. After a while, she spoke up to translate our English. This was Kilo.

We were in a Zemba village that, in spite of sitting not ten miles through roadless savanna from the nearest town, had never before hosted a group of tourists. They had no water, no electricity. Their huts were built of twigs and mud. Chunks of squash cooked over an open fire. Children, mostly naked, played in the dirt. The adults moved about languidly or sat around the fire.

We had previously visited a range of different tribes: Nhoma Bushmen, who hunt naked and click while talking; the Himba in Kaokoland, whose women wear brief cattle-hide skirts and only jewelry above the waist; their distantly related Herrera, converted by early missionaries to

Christianity, wearing elaborate Victorian dress. Unlike this Zemba village, all of them benefitted from occasional visits by tourists.

The Zemba are also distantly related to the better-known Himba. This particular tribe was forced to flee to Angola during the wars that ended with Namibia's freedom in the late 1980s. The Zemba returned here, to northern Namibia near the town of Opuwo. The elaborate cattle-hide skirts of the Himba had evolved to colorful cloth wraps in this group; but they retained their characteristic colored beads. Likewise, the women's naked breasts—regardless of size or sag—still gleamed proudly in the sun.

Everyone in the small village was closely related to the chief—Tuayamapi Tjiuana—a tall, thin, eighty-seven-year-old man wearing an old blue sporting jacket from some church's donation bin. His serene, penetrating gaze observed his world in silence. There was a depth to his eyes and a calm gentleness to his face that seemed improbable after surviving the hardships of half a lifetime of war in this impoverished land.

Kilo lived with her Grandmother Muponge. Grandmother's eyes were strong but held something in reserve. Her body was firm and almost masculine, but for breasts that bore testimony to motherhood. I suspected she was close to my own sixty-six years, but couldn't begin to imagine being in her shoes—or lack of them. She protectively stood to the right of the chief, while his other wife stood to the left, creating an aura of strength and caring.

Kilo's mother was a hardy woman who left every evening before dark to sleep in a field of maize that needed protection from roaming herds of cattle. Before leaving the village, my group promised to return and bring her a blanket for the cold nights.

At one time it must have seemed to Kilo that her future was full of promise, for she was lucky enough to live with an aunt in Windhoek, Namibia's capital, and go to school. In her final year there, she met a young man, got pregnant, and had to return to her village. She was now raising an impetuous, vibrant young girl. Kilo's face and arms spoke of a lithe beauty, but—unlike her fellow tribeswomen—her body was covered by a well-worn blue and white dress. She, along with her mother and daughter, were among the few whose breasts would not be on public view again; attending school had instilled in her a modesty not shown by the other women, who had not succumbed to the influence of the missionaries.

The little girl's father, I learned, went to India to study shortly after the child's conception.

"Will you join him when he returns?" I asked, regretting the question almost immediately.

Kilo's eyes shifted past me before she answered.

"No. This is my village. I will always be here… This is my home. I will always be here."

She spoke without any inflection. No resignation. No anger. No emotion. But there was a power to her words that spoke of survival. Of deep attachment. Of simultaneously living and observing her own life. So much said with so few words.

"This is my home. I will always be here."

The word "promiscuity" is heard often when describing Zemba culture, but in a manner mostly free of judgment. There is little concept of men having ownership of or exclusivity with women. It seems wives of the same husband bear no resentment toward each other. Children, their parentage unquestioned, are cared for by the entire tribe.

While much about the culture was comforting for Kilo and her daughter, Kilo had been on a divergent path, integrating into a radically different world. I struggled to imagine her returning to this lifestyle, from an earlier century. When I realized she was carrying yet another child, a degree of hopelessness settled on me.

As I considered Kilo's future, my own past pulled at me. My family left my birthland, Yugoslavia, when I was a child. I revisited it as a young woman and knew, unlike Kilo, that it was no longer my home. The depth of Kilo's connection to her home was in stark contrast with my own path. She had accepted her place. I could not imagine going back.

Kilo translated the chief's plea for medication to ease the pain in his old joints. Then she explained that a great-aunt had a bad gash and infection on her foot, caused during the night by getting too close to the fire in her cold, mud hut. We gave her some antibiotic cream and told her to boil water and wash the foot before putting the cream on.

"Do it just before she goes to bed," I said, imagining the woman curling under a blanket—only to then recall it was the very lack of a blanket that got the old woman, her emaciated ancient frame devoid of warming fat, into her predicament.

"We will come back in the morning with medicated cream, some pills for your grandfather's pain, and a blanket," I said.

Kilo looked at me for a long time without saying anything. It occurred to me that this was a young woman who had waited more than once for someone to return who never did.

I wrapped my hand around her shoulder, looked her in the eye, and said, "I will be back in the morning. I promise."

"I am starting to think you might be someone unique," she finally said.

We moved toward her mother, who was calling us over for a photograph she desperately wanted us to take.

The following morning we were on the road early. We arrived in the nearby town of Opuwo before the stores opened. A nearly characterless mix of rickety old shacks amid cheap modern structures, there were a few grocery stores, gas stations, and banks, as well as a post office thrown in for good measure. The town stretched for a couple of miles on the road near the Angola border. Himba, Zemba, Herero, Angolans, and contemporarily dressed Namibians passed in groups that did not mix but also did not conflict. The nearly naked stuck together, as did the elaborately garbed, both recalling worlds long disappeared in the rest of our universe, to the early tribal and the Victorian.

At seven-thirty we pleaded with the employees of a large shop to open early.

"We just need two blankets," said our guide.

"No! Get six!" I cried.

The clerk just shrugged and glanced at his boss in back of the store.

Nothing.

As we started to drive off in despair, someone called out. We turned back to find the door to the store was open.

The clerk welcomed us in.

I rushed around, frantically grabbing baby clothes and a large tent-like black-and-white striped dress. We got the blankets, medicine, and two pairs of size seven sneakers. Our guide grabbed a pair of fluffy socks for the infected foot.

As we drove off, I regretted that we didn't buy more blankets. More shoes. More everything.

Back in the village, the chief was overwhelmed by our haul. The blankets were apportioned to the elders—although we made sure one was held back for Kilo's mother, who was still out in the fields. I was relieved to hear our guide tell the chief that he would bring another group of tourists in a few weeks. They would bring more blankets. Our guide had not found an untouristed village in a long time, and he promised to tell others about this one.

A subtle shift had started. This village would never be the same again.

Before we said our goodbyes, I sat by the fire as Kilo's male cousin finished making me a wood bowl. I watched, savoring every step of the process, which colored pale wood ochre and black. A woman joined in, pounding a rust-colored powder into the wood, polishing it. I watched Kilo's cousin as he reheated a wide blade between every burnishing, using it to replicate patterns his ancestors designed in an earlier millennium. I took home not a simple wood bowl, but a memory of the loving care with which it was finished.

Once the bowl was complete, I pulled Kilo aside and handed her a bag. She looked at the contents and sighed.

"So you know I am pregnant?"

She was visibly relieved. A Western perspective had colored her self-image, making it difficult for her to tell me, unprompted.

"Oh, yes," I replied. "When is it due?"

The baby was a boy, due in one month. He would be born in town. His father—like his sibling's—was now out of the picture. I learned that prenatal care was free, but Grandmother Muponge would pay for the birthing from her government-provided pension of around $80 a month, the only regular income in the village at that time.

I told Kilo I wished I could know when the baby was born, a seemingly idle hope.

"Do you have Snapchat?" she asked.

I was stunned. I told her I was unfamiliar with Snapchat, but wondered if she was on Facebook.

"Of course."

Surrounded by naked breasts, we discussed social media as if we were in a Silicon Valley coffee shop, as opposed to a tribal village.

Kilo finally opened up. She told me that when her baby was born she would go into town and apply for a job. She would finish school. She thought she could be a good nurse. I believed she could, and hoped she had the strength to make her dream reality. I felt better after this, our final conversation. Aspiration could live here, along with hopes for a better future.

"But how can she access Facebook?" friends on my expedition asked later.

I had no idea. We ourselves could barely access it in this backwater, even in hotels that claimed to provide Wi-Fi.

The same afternoon, wandering on a hilltop in that remote northern desert of Namibia, I found a spot with a weak cellular signal, seemingly the only one for miles around. I jabbed my iPhone, my finger cracking from dirt and dryness. My actions were almost robotic:

Log onto Facebook.
Find the Search field.
Type "Kilo K."
Wait.
Get exactly one match.
Select it.
See a familiar face.

Kilo's life was unimaginably different from mine. But our connection, impossible to foresee, somehow felt inevitable. I was far closer in age to Kilo's beloved Grandmother Muponge; but the chasm between Grandmother Muponge and me was yet another quantum leap deeper. Kilo and I at least shared a language. And technology.

Kilo is a young woman whose story reached something in me that by now should have been inaccessibly protected, shut down like an overflowing inbox. There are over a billion people on this Earth in situations hardly different from hers. There are untold numbers of girls who have traded their futures for a warm body next to theirs.

Yet it was our specific paths that had crossed. Something deep in Kilo reached out to me, and we touched each other across an unimaginable divide, a canyon deeper and wider than the Grand. I almost felt despair at her fate, but there was a strength in her that prevented that. I wanted a connection, a link to this young woman in a dirt-floored village. I wanted to believe that she would move into her own future. I wanted to watch, even from afar.

I sent the friend request.

22 HIMBA AND HERERO

Two groups populate the remote northwest part of Namibia near the village of Purro. Trite expressions like "chalk and cheese" come to mind in describing the Himba and Herero. They share dark-black skin and an apparent common ancestry, and the two groups peacefully coexist in this barren desert land. But it would be hard to mistake one for the other.

The Himba live in tiny, round huts built of twigs and covered with cow dung and random bits of cloth. The Herero also use dried cow dung to build their homes; but they favor tiny rectangular houses much smaller than a typical trailer. What's more, the Herero have found a Christian god, so a church sits squarely amid their structures.

Although both groups are incredibly classy in their garb, their style of dress could hardly be more different.

The Himba wander nearly naked, breasts glowing and legs bare. Their butts are covered with wonderful furry brown strips of domesticated stock—primarily cow or the quirky-looking goat-sheep. Their legs and arms are covered in metal bracelets, and their necks are wrapped in layers of necklaces made from bits of polished ostrich eggs and porcupine quills. Everything—skin, hair, and leather covering—is coated in a layer of red powder made by scraping a stone the color of dried blood—called an *okla*—on rough rock. This lends the Himba an otherworldly glow, as well as protection against sun, insects, and body odors.

The Herero, taught by nineteenth-century missionaries to forsake their lewd nakedness, wander this same barren desert dressed as if Alice in Wonderland grew up to have a perpetual tea party with the Mad Hatter. Voluminous ruffled skirts cover bellies whose ideal form, I was told, is the hippo—preferably well rounded to demonstrate wealth. The frame that forms the shape to meet a lady's fancy is a coat hanger lifted from milady's dresser. Jewelry is minimal, but headdress seems mandatory. Imagine a visit to Ascot in high season, where, rather than crafted in the finest London shops, the hats are the handiwork of a remote desert milliner. Instead of birds perched on blond locks, a form of cattle horns perch over glowing black cheeks. Colors are bold, patterns vibrant, and designs seem unchanged from the days when the Christians arrived and the Victorian style still flourished.

The Himba and Herero may be at the same party, but they got drastically different memos about the dress code.

23 CONNECTING AND CLICKING

A skinny man sped towards me, navigating the rough track in the pale light of morning. He jerked up—startled, no doubt, by my fancy trail shoes—then stared at my white face. An excited set of words filled with clicks flew at me. I listened, entranced, but could only respond with a smile, an offer of a handshake, and a greeting in my own language. We parted, heading in opposite directions, but glancing backwards a few times, in regret of the missed opportunity to communicate more deeply.

I was traveling through a remote part of South Africa, in an area once called Zululand, when I first started focusing on the "clicking" in the local speech. I loved the clicks and tried to emulate them, but instead only managed to muster insipid wet-smack sounds. They could have been cartoon kisses, maybe a *tsk, tsk*, despite my best intentions, an insult to the very concept of clicks as part of language.

I consider myself skilled at learning languages, however, and was not ready to give up.

I sat for hours in a rattling four-wheel drive as we navigated through the countryside, practicing the fancy mouth work. I finally found a snap at the back of my jaw that clicked with a beautiful resonance. I was thrilled and worked it carefully. It got louder as I felt it echo through my mouth.

"That's very insulting," our driver and guide, Lungelo, finally said. He had been warm and gracious until then. His comment startled me.

"What do you mean?" I asked.

It turned out the particular click I had perfected had a meaning that Lungelo was too polite to translate.

The next morning I started practicing my clicking again, trying for something less offensive.

"*Crick.*" Pause. "*Crack.*" Longer recovery break. "*Crick.*"

Lungelo cracked up.

"You've got it to a *t*," he said, still not telling me what it meant. "Even those who don't understand Zulu, if they live in South Africa, they will understand you."

"Does it mean 'fuck off'?" I asked.

"Not that bad!" he exclaimed. "It means 'piss off' or 'leave me alone'!"

I continued practicing. Lungelo roared with laughter every time I got it.

"It starts at the upper left. I round my mouth, close my lips, and push out toward the right," I explained. Lungelo looked amused and agreed.

There are several languages in which I only know curse words. I once had a boss from Holland. He spent hours on the phone speaking to the woman with whom he was in the middle of an acrimonious divorce. My Dutch is dangerous.

In Serbian, my mother tongue, I was eighteen before I heard my first swear word. It is a language where curses are frequently interspersed in conversation, especially by the men; but I learned it from my mother, a woman too gracious to ever utter one. I had to wait for a trip to Serbia to understand what was missing from my vocabulary.

Now I needed to learn something more positive to say in Zulu.

Lungelo tried to teach me the word for kissing, *qanula*. I couldn't quite master the *q* click, no matter how hard I tried.

"What about 'I love you'?" I wondered.

"There isn't a click for that," he replied.

I didn't know if it was true or just his way of preventing me from clicking love messages to goat herders throughout the countryside.

I feared I would leave Zululand knowing only one local expression well: "Piss off!"

I finally stopped practicing and never used my expertise in public. While Lungelo assured me it would be understood if I ever needed it, all the people I interacted with were gracious and warm. I had much more use for smiles than clicks.

A few days later, my travel companions and I stayed in a local family's home in Zululand, near the border with an area known as the Wild Coast. The surrounding scrub-covered hills were spotted with makeshift households. Each had a few small buildings, and they often featured an outhouse holding pride of place smack in the middle of the best viewpoint. Next to the outhouses lay the graves of departed loved ones, whose pictures also adorned living room walls.

Offering home stays represented a way out of poverty, and the houses improved as more guests came. Local nonprofits helped manage the tourist infrastructure and encouraged guides to bring customers. All the same, tourists were still very rare. We saw none in our entire time in the area.

The home we were staying in was quite comfortable. It had running water and flush toilets, closer to my expectations of a bed-and-breakfast than a homestay, where you might sleep on the floor and share an outhouse. It was run by the women of a family who had inherited the property from their grandfather, and all the work was done by family members. There were several large bedrooms, and the family told me they could all sleep in one to free up the others when guests arrived.

In their culture, single daughters stayed on in the household, and the oldest son brought his family there. Perhaps there were still men in the family, but I never saw or heard about any.

I also learned that if children were born to single women, the women's mothers took responsibility for the babies. For life! I am still struggling to make sense of that. I fear I might have been observing the beginning of a women's revolution of sorts, one where a lot more young mothers skip marriage and selfishly foist responsibility for raising their illegitimate children upon their elders. It makes martyrs of today's generation of grandmothers, who have already spent a lifetime working to pick up the slack of those around them, especially the males. Unfortunately these young women were learning from the examples of their fathers, uncles, and grandfathers. My awareness raised, I observed the phenomenon elsewhere throughout the country.

One morning some days later, I woke as chickens started crowing shortly before daybreak. I rose quietly and, as the roosters calmed, the sun rose, and the birds started chirping, I headed out to explore.

That morning and over the next two, I made several new friends at a most unlikely spot: the neighborhood water spigot, a brief walk up the dirt road from where we were staying. It turned out ours was the only house in the village that had piped in running water.

I was talking to my new friend, young Thandeka—who lived nearby and was carrying six large buckets to her house—when she turned to greet an elderly gentleman I had already met a little way up the trail. He and I had shaken hands and connected, as much as possible with no common language. But Thandeka spoke English, and I was excited to learn a little more about the man.

"Who was that?" I asked after he left.

"Oh, that was Mistapha."

A few repetitions later I realized she was saying Mister Hlophe. He was her grandfather.

"But what do you call him? Don't you say 'grandfather'?"

"Yes, I call him Mkhulu. That is 'grandfather' in Zulu," she explained. "Do you speak Zulu?"

Aha! A chance to use my language skills. I had not dared try to speak Zulu with the elderly gentleman; but now I concentrated, wanting to get my one click word right.

"*Crick!*" I said.

Thandeka's eyes opened wide.

I repeated, "*Crick!*"

Thandeka roared with laughter, confirming with a hand motion that I had successfully said "piss off."

"Do you know any more?" she asked.

"Anything more polite, you mean? No, it's my only Zulu word."

We almost rolled over laughing, which was dangerous, since Thandeka was carrying twenty-five liters of water—weighing two pounds a liter—in a yellow bucket on her head.

I thought about Thandeka the rest of the day.

The next morning I stepped out to take Thandeka a gift, one of the little flashlights I carry with me on trips.

I found her at home, maybe a hundred yards downhill from the spigot, already washing clothes, but happy to take a break. She loved the flashlight and agreed to take a selfie with me—but only after she wrapped her hair in a pink cloth, as she was not, in her mind, perfectly coiffed.

We were surrounded by rough dirt hills that dropped down to the creeks that wove their way throughout the territory. Homes were scattered about haphazardly. Most seemed in some stage of repair—or disrepair. Metal roofs were replacing thatch, rectangular structures replacing the traditional round forms. Goats and chickens ran around. I could wander at will on foot, but traversing this area by car was nearly impossible on the rugged dirt tracks.

On my way back up the hill from Thandeka's, as I was passing the water spigot again, I met Daphne, a fifty-four-year-old, just as effortlessly flipping about fifty pounds of water onto her head as the young woman had. I couldn't resist another conversation. Once we had chatted, I wanted to give her a flashlight as well. She was on her way before I had a chance, so I followed her home.

Daphne didn't mind if I walked home with her, but warned me that her house was "not very nice."

We walked past Thandeka's house, then veered to the left onto a narrow trail. It sloped gently downward at first, then grew rough, watermarked, and steep. Trying to keep up, I feared I would slip and break my leg. She laughed and talked, stopping and turning around, heavy bucket swaying, to make sure I was keeping up. Determined, I finally made it to the bottom.

Daphne again took a left, pausing to point out a concrete structure.

"Soon that will be my new home."

"Really?"

"Yes," she said proudly. "The government is building it for me."

We crossed a few boards over a swampy spot, soon

after which we reached her current home. It was a small old whitewashed rectangle with a metal roof. Daphne had to turn sideways so the water barrel would fit through the door.

Inside was crowded but neat. The only table, small and round, held an iron and a blue pair of men's pants. A young boy, Daphne's grandson, sat on a torn old sofa that ran the length of most of one wall, breakfast on his lap. Across from him, on a cot that served as their bed, sat Daphne's husband, wearing a blue shirt and wrapped in an old orange towel instead of pants. He was eating some porridge and an ear of dried corn, while reading a newspaper. Both males stared at me with mild surprise. Neither rose to help Daphne with her load.

Daphne was terribly excited and called repeatedly to her three daughters to join us. They were in bed behind a small door and couldn't be bothered to get up.

Her son, a handsome young man we had seen outside, came in to chat. He wore a U.S. Polo Association T-shirt. I visualized a lady in the American South shoving secondhand clothing into her church's contribution basket, shaking her head at the waste of this nearly new item in her son's drawer. I doubt she could have envisioned its final resting place, but it was certainly appreciated here.

Daphne joined her husband on the bed so I could take a picture, but it felt very stiff. Looking for a laugh to get them to relax, I tried my Zulu.

"*Crick*," I clicked, again working hard to get my one click right.

Daphne and her husband both roared with laughter. Hard to believe, but it worked every time.

We talked a bit more, before I needed to get back for breakfast.

When I was ready to leave, Daphne came with me. She had one more water container to bring down from the spigot.

On the climb back up the hill, Daphne told me more about her life. I learned that she was responsible for all the water for the family. She cooked all the food. She shopped. She cleaned the house. She washed the clothes. She ironed.

She fed the chickens. All this with no electricity or running water.

"What does everyone else do?"

"Sometimes they help."

"I bet it's not very often," I said lightheartedly, though actually I wasn't joking.

Daphne sheepishly confirmed they didn't help very often. But she never stopped smiling and laughing as we continued up the steep hill. Daphne had no time for self-pity; just time to care for her world.

"Does your husband work?"

"No, there are no jobs." At this she did look sad.

"Do your daughters or your son work?" They were adults in their twenties and thirties, all single. By now I knew that meant Daphne was also responsible for the grandchildren.

"No, there are no jobs."

I wondered why young Thandeka could carry six pails of water and wash clothes, while Daphne's daughters lounged about; but, I had to let it go.

As we passed Daphne's new house, I learned that the government builds houses for poor people, and that she had signed up six years earlier for the program. The house would have two bedrooms, a living room, a kitchen, and a bathroom. It would be finished in a few months, and Daphne was very excited about the move. We would see a fair number of these government-issue homes, maybe six hundred square feet in size, in our travels.

I was Daphne's first American visitor. She asked about my husband and children and grandchildren. She hoped I liked her country. Unlike me, she was too circumspect to poke questions at my lifestyle, and I was too embarrassed at the differences in our circumstances to volunteer anything. Instead, I plunged recklessly ahead with my own questions.

"Will you have water in the new house?" I almost hated to hear the answer.

"No," she said.

"I'm sorry…"

"But," she interrupted, "I am saving money and will run a pipe from the spigot to the house."

"Do you have a job?" Since no one else in her family worked, I had assumed she didn't either.

"Yes, I take care of the old people." She had a government job at a home for the elderly. To get there, she walked and took one of the pervasive mini cab taxis for almost an hour each way.

"So you do everything in your house, you take care of everyone, and you have a job. The only job in the family."

"Yes ma'am," she beamed.

All too soon for me, we were back at the spigot.

"This gift is tiny," I said, handing her the small flashlight.

She fingered the light, pointed at a dark corner, and said, "It is tiny, but it is not a small gift."

My interaction with Daphne touched my heart. I couldn't stop thinking about her as I headed back to breakfast in the comfort of my homestay. I knew the recollection of her strength, her smile, and her determination would stay with me for a long time. She had no Internet or Facebook; we would not stay connected. But her story would not let me be.

I had to help get that water to her house.

The second time I approached the narrow trail down the steep slope to Daphne's house, I was alone. I couldn't make it even part way. My fear of falling got worse with every step. I stopped just below the top of the hill and shouted her name several times. She appeared from the house and sped up the hill toward me.

We hugged, and I slipped money into her hand. Upon seeing just one of the denominations, she burst into tears. So did I.

We hugged again. And again.

I made her promise me two things: one, that she would tell no one of my gift; and two, that she would make her children work.

She promised both.

I made her repeat the second promise.

She did and then, with a big smile, she broke into a torrent of words in her own language, interspersed with clicks.

If I had just had a little bit more time, I know I would have learned the click for "I love you."

24 SAMBURU SOFTENING

I sit deep in a Samburu hut built of twigs, old cloth, ripped cardboard, and random debris. Ordinarily, dung would be used as covering, but the current lack of local grazing has pushed the cattle so far away that dung is in short supply. The head of the family—who also happens to be the village chief—sits watching me. His face closed, he observes without any affect or emotion.

From outside, the four-foot tall structure looks tiny; inside there are three areas, as well as a cook fire at the far end of the entry. A couple and babies sleep in one cattle-hide-lined compartment, young people in the other. The men rest their heads on triangular pieces of wood, while a woman my age confesses to a pillow I spy in a corner.

In the village, women build the homes, clean the surroundings, tend the goats, cook the food, and bear and care for the children. The men sit in deep, serious discussion, debating matters of state. Despite the women's disproportionate share of responsibilities, the men are the rulers of the roost.

Light from the hut entrance turns the regal face before

me a deep bronze, lighting the interior so I can use my phone to snap a photo. I show the man his portrait and feel a slight thaw. I flip the camera to selfie mode and place the phone in his hand. He stares at it, shifts it about, and finally sees his own face staring back. I gently reach for a finger on his other hand and feel its muscles release. Together, the man and I try to push the large white button, but instead our jerky motion moves the focus. I try again, then push the playback button.

The man's face eases a bit more as he looks at his image.

Soon he has grasped the concept and is satisfied with the results. He grins when reviewing the pictures we've taken, but prefers a serious self image.

A baby wanders into the hut, followed by a young child, both of whom make their way into the photo frame. When observers block the doorway, it's hard to explain to the man that it's too dark to shoot. But the crowd is too thick to clear.

The chief stands up and walks off with my phone, bestowing a view of the image on his court. He is beaming when he returns the device, and holds my hand for a long moment as I say "*Lesere*," in farewell.

"*Ashoalei*," he says.

Thank you.

TANIA ROMANOV

25 ANGRY ANCESTORS

My ancestors are angry.

Mama Zulu, a Sangoma who was communicating with my ancestors, issued an aggressive series of shrieks punctuated with exclamations. Had I been an ancestor, I might have run the other direction. Clearly the Sangomas were not warm and fuzzy when communicating with the departed.

Sangomas are traditional healers in Southern Africa. Some Sangomas spend their lives in traditional religious communities, including the Shembe church, the preeminent denomination in Zulu communities.

Sangomas are called to their work by ancestors, a call that may not be refused. Those called must either comply or risk serious illness—or even death. Sangomas might be older when the calling comes. It might come through an illness that teaches them the path.

Regardless of when the calling is received, it always

involves communication with ancestors. Serious training follows, including instruction in locally found herbal medicines. The South African government even offers qualified Sangomas certification in their dispensation.

South Africa has around 25,000 medical doctors and 200,000 Sangomas. Up to sixty percent of the population visits the Sangomas, who often work in concert with doctors. No serious Sangoma would tell someone to stop seeing their medical practitioner.

These traditional healers worked their way into our consciousness as my friends and I traversed South Africa. Eventually we could almost recognize the Sangomas on sight as they walked through the countryside. Soon we were searching them out.

Fascinated, we listened to the stories of how the Sangomas we met came to their practices, which they took very seriously. In the process, we came to respect them, making it impossible for us to ignore their messages.

As we came across Sangomas, my friends and I took turns having our ancestors addressed. One Sangoma told my friend she would suffer vision problems and risked going blind. The woman went on to talk of my friend losing feeling in her left side—at which point my friend stopped the translation. She couldn't bear to hear more. She passed on being the subject of any further visions.

Several Sangomas spoke to my friend Nevada of her sore hips. All recommended avoiding surgery, which she had been actively considering. One offered a healing herbal solution. With loud rasping whines, another, older and more experienced, shared the pain Nevada's ancestors felt, surprising us when she reemerged from her trance by declaring that Nevada was very lucky. Her luck, however, was at risk. Nevada's paternal grandmother one was the one responsible for her good fortune, but she was feeling neglected. She needed to be thanked and, through ceremony, made aware of her granddaughter's appreciation.

Mama Zulu had lit three large candles and stuck them into the sand. We sat on the ground. She pulled me to her, so we were facing each other, and lit two more candles. She pushed one into my hand, keeping the other in hers, then wrapped my hands in a death grip. Meanwhile, a hive of bees swarmed in the broken window behind her head, the insects swirling in the smoke and buzzing with a frightening intensity.

Mama Zulu started chanting. I stared, mesmerized by her face and the flames.

She continued chanting. The longer she chanted, the more the candles bent from the pressure of our hands. All I could concentrate on was the crown of melted wax atop the candle. Soon drops started falling—first onto Mama Zulu's hand, then mine. Following Mama Zulu's lead, I ignored the searing pain. Conversation with the ancestors was not to be interrupted for something so minor.

Then came the message.

My ancestors were angry.

In fact, they were furious with me. Having neglected and ignored their fury, I was causing untold grief.

Before I had a chance to make a rational decision about whether I believed the message, despair overtook my body. I could not take this anger from my ancestors lightly.

But which ancestors?

My mother? Was I mistaken in my belief that we had been on beautiful terms before she died? My father? Was I wrong to think our pain had healed in the years since his death?

Mama Zulu continued.

The anger was about an inheritance, a will.

As soon as I heard that, I figured the information was actually for the friend sitting next to me. Her mother had recently died. The estate was still in dispute.

All the same, something told me there was more to it—something for me. I kept turning over Mama Zulu's words in my mind.

Driving through the countryside one day, along a dirt road we saw two women sitting in the shade, next to a large pile of branches. The women were resting, having gone a long way downriver to pick herbs for local Sangomas to use in their healing.

One pile was so heavy I could not lift it. Energized by an apple we gave her—as if that were somehow all it took—a Sangoma named Thenjiwe easily hoisted the pile onto her shoulder. I was impressed.

We learned that the heavy pile would be used to treat stomachache. What the other was to be used for was harder to understand, the discussion finally resorting to a lot of pointing at backsides.

We finally figured out the lighter pile was for enemas.

Another very experienced Sangoma, Livumile, was interrupted in her work with my friend Nevada at the insistence of a very tall white man who wanted to comfort me.

Learning that my late husband, Harold, was extremely tall, Livumile talked to me about issues with his family. She saw a male and female child; Harold had a son and daughter, my stepchildren. Livumile wanted to hold something that belonged to them, but was able to work from a picture instead.

It would take me a while to understand the message Harold was trying to pass on. But as I kept traveling and listening, I eventually would.

Another issue that remained unresolved involved a white necklace. Livumile insisted it had some sort of significance. I had no idea what.

While exploring some hot sulfur pits one morning, my friends and I met a large family who had spent four days and nights helping launch a new Sangoma on her path.

We listened to rhythmic chanting somewhere deep in the nearby forest, the final phase of the Sangoma's initiation. Because of the cold, I had put on my down jacket. Most of the family was wrapped in thick blankets. We waited for the new Sangoma.

Suddenly, she emerged from the jungle—nearly naked, despite the cold!

She had left her old identity behind. The ancestors gave her no choice but to appear naked in this very spot to start her new life of healing.

It was my turn again when we sat with Thelma, a sixty-eight-year-old Sangoma. Not only did she have a powerful presence, we quickly discovered that she also had a mastery of ritual unrivaled by anyone we had seen until then.

Thelma wore colorful wraps, plentiful beadwork, and on her legs hundreds of bangles made of metal bottle caps. The noise of the clanking as she danced combined with the pounding of a large drum by her grandson, keening by her granddaughter, and her own high-pitched chanting.

We sat on the floor of a *rondevel*, or roundhouse. This one was larger than most we had visited, perhaps twenty feet in diameter. It had a traditional thatched roof, under which the noise resounded. Lit candles and burning herbs leant an ethereal quality to the scene, as Thelma stepped onto the platter of burning herbs over and over. I could hardly pull my eyes away from her feet. Only when I managed to do so did I realize that she showed no signs of pain, focused as she was on her intense interchange with the ancestors.

Thelma moved closer. Before I knew it, she was poking and pushing and pulling at me. My back. My neck. My legs, feet, and arms. Then she wrapped her arms around my head. While still embracing me, she talked of headaches and foot cramps, both correct. She removed my glasses and rolled her thumbs around my eyes, firmly but without causing pain.

"I can help your vision," she said in closing.

Thelma offered to make a necklace to restore clear vision to my nearsighted eyes. I readily accepted, and she got started. I watched for a few moments, then went outside to leave her to her work.

When she was finished a short while later, I looked at the necklace: a string of white beads. I took off my glasses and put the necklace around my neck.

After a few days, I realized that without my glasses I was seeing buildings and workers and trees—even leaves—that, until then, I had been unable to see without my corrective lenses. It could have been a trick, whether of Thelma's or my own mind; either way, I was happy to play along.

My own ancestors finally penetrated my fog.

The ancestors with whom Mama Zulu had communicated didn't have to be my parents. The situation to which she had alluded could go back much further.

My thoughts were guided toward a situation my brother Sasha and I had stumbled upon a few years earlier. We were visiting our mother's homeland, so I could research my book, *Mother Tongue*.

I now understood that it was my great grandfather, whose grave I had recently visited, who was hurt that his descendants were still angry over his legacy, the distribution of which they bitterly disputed.

My brother and I learned about the dispute when visiting the house where my mother was born. My grandfather fled Mussolini's takeover of Istria, now part of Croatia, but his lands were eventually returned to his descendants. His sister's family felt they should have gone to them rather than to our side of the family, and the bitterness lingered. Sasha and I were scorned at the cemetery for being on the wrong side, even though we were unaware of the dispute and had turned down our inheritance. We tried to get the feuding family members—who lived within a mile of each other—together but ran out of time.

Mama Zulu thought there was an ocean and ships involved. My great grandfather lived on the sea and was a shipbuilder. She insisted I should bring my family together at the sea and celebrate with as many of them as possible.

By the time I headed for home in California, something

had clarified inside me. I understood that my new necklace was intended for my grandson, Baker. There was a direct link from my tall husband to this very tall young man, a link Sangoma Livumile must have seen while I was still blinded.

I also came to understand that it wasn't my eyesight Sangoma Thelma was focused on; it was my ability to see and understand the world around me in new ways.

The next time I visited Baker in Colorado, I offered him the necklace. I was hesitant, self-conscious he would find bizarre the notion of a medicine woman in Africa wanting him to have this necklace. When I was a fifteen-year-old teenager, I'm not sure how I would have reacted in a similar situation.

Much to my surprise, Baker understood immediately. Not only did he readily accept the gift, he went with his mom to have it repaired and adjusted. Now he wears it all the time. I hope he carries the comfort of his grandfather's love with him through life.

As for Mother Zulu's insight about Croatia, I followed her advice: I gathered my extended family where my mother was born. Kids, grandkids, siblings, cousins, second cousins—you name it, they were there. One side of the family assured me the other would not come; in the end everyone gathered for a joyous and loving reunion.

I was brought up in a very religious Christian community, but it didn't stick. Over the course of my life, I passed through various forms of spirituality, from Russian mystics like Gurdjieff to Sufism. I watched meditation restore my husband when he struggled with an illness that eventually led to his passing.

Over the last few years I have come to understand that there are inexplicable powers that help guide me through my life. I find them in some of the most remote and unexpected places. The only thing I know for sure is that I need to be open to hearing their voices.

The Sangomas reminded me of that.

26 EARLY MORNING RAIN

A massive bulk crossed our path so swiftly we might not have even noticed, if it weren't for the arm of our guide waving wildly at us to follow him.

"Run! Run!" he shouted.

Suddenly we were all fleeing through the bush, away from the river. The bulk—a hippo—briefly veered towards the gun pointed at it, then changed course, crashing through the underbrush and continuing to the water. Breaking branches and loud splashes shattered the morning silence. My heart pounded.

A few months earlier, in California, I had told a friend about this trip.

"You're going to walk across Africa? Are you out of your effing mind!"

"I'm not walking across Africa. I'm just walking across Tsavo Park in Kenya. It's a two-week walk. I think it'll be wonderful."

"Oh yeah! Just you and the lions and elephants and cheetahs, right?"

She forgot to mention the hippos and crocodiles. In all

fairness, at that time I can't say I was very aware of them either.

"Yes! Doesn't it sound exciting?"

"Do the people organizing the trip know how old you are?"

"Well, the leader was our guide when Harold and I climbed Mount Kenya more than fifteen years ago. I suspect he doesn't think I got younger since then."

"Yeah, well..."

"I'm only mentioning the trip because I thought you might want to come. My brother Alex and my friend Judy are coming, and you always seem interested in my travels."

"Maybe invite me on a different trip. Didn't I read something recently about terrorist attacks in Kenya? Some problems in the north, along the coast and in Nairobi?"

I hadn't even mentioned we were ending on Lamu, a small island off the north coast of Kenya, near the Somalia border. I decided this was not the time to bring it up.

"You probably did. But you can't worry about all that stuff, or you'd never go anywhere."

The first time I visited Kenya was in the early 1980s. My most recent trip was in 1997 with a few friends and my husband Harold, shortly after his diagnosis with cancer.

We went a little crazy that first year of his illness. We skied into a tenth-mountain-division hut in the Rockies to celebrate New Year's with a group of friends. We circumnavigated Annapurna in the Himalayas of Nepal. We explored the canyons of Utah. We spent a month in Kenya, visiting wild game preserves and hiking to the top of 17,000-foot tall Mount Kenya. We played for a week in Paris, then fell in love with the coast of Italy below Genoa.

We skied for two months in Vail, Colorado. We believed we only had a couple of years to enjoy the world together, and we intended to make the most of them.

Later that same year, we heard about guide Iain Allen leading a group of people to the top of Kilimanjaro, after which they walked from the base of the mountain all the way to Mombasa on the coast of Kenya. It triggered our imaginations, but we never did anything about it while Harold was still alive.

On my own now, I kept walking, sometimes almost obsessively. It was the only way I knew to keep moving forward into a life without Harold.

I signed up for the Walk Across Africa. It was timed to coincide with the end of the dry season. Alex and I left from San Francisco, landing in Paris for our connecting flight. As we waited, reports of a terrorist attack on a shopping mall came on the news screen in the waiting area. It was September 21, 2013. The shopping mall was in Nairobi, Kenya. It was a major attack, and the news shocked the world as we prepared to board.

I texted Iain: "Should we still come?"

"Of course. The mall is on the other end of the city from our hotel."

In the press, it sounded as if the entire country were on lockdown. We saw images of police and soldiers out in force around Nairobi. There were casualties, explosions, and smoke. Some people were escaping, while others were being taken hostage inside the Westgate Mall.

The fact that our hotel was on the other end of town did not exactly reassure us.

Should we still go? Alex and I asked each other.

We decided there was no point in second-guessing the situation. We boarded the plane to Nairobi. Given another day to mull it over, I am not sure what we would have done. Many safaris over the next weeks were cancelled. Kenya suffered from a huge drop in tourist revenues.

The streets of Nairobi were deserted when we arrived. They remained so the next day. We went to another shopping mall to replace a camera Alex had lost at an airport security check. As we walked in, the camera store was closing due to safety concerns, as was the entire mall. It turned out that the attack was ongoing, and the army had the Westgate Mall—where the attack had taken place—surrounded. We also learned the attack was a reprisal by al-Shabaab for Kenyan military involvement in Somalia. It was impossible to think or talk about anything else.

We left the next morning, the crisis still unresolved. For the next two weeks we would worry about wild animals, not terrorists.

Including Alex, Judy, and myself, there were eight Americans on our trek. Three Samburu tribesmen and two white Kenyans made up the rest of our group.

Every detail of our trip was carefully planned to ensure a smooth journey through the wilderness. We worked hard to leave no trace and not to disturb any animals. A little over a century ago, when escaped slaves were briefly plentiful, the lions of this region learned to eat people. The legend of those Man Eaters of Tsavo persists, but the lions here paid little or no attention to us.

All the same, our guides carried guns. Large guns. However, their objective was to never use them. Iain was an honorary park ranger and the only person allowed to bring walkers into Tsavo. He respected his role as a game warden and protector, and told us that, if he ever had to kill an elephant, he would terminate these trips. There were

13,000 elephants in Tsavo's 8,000 square miles, and Iain was in love with each one, gentle giants being savagely poached all across Africa for their ivory.

Neither lions nor elephants, though, represented the biggest threat on this two-week walking safari—from within sight of Kilimanjaro to near Mombasa on the coast. We had now come face-to-face with it: the 5,000-pound hippo that had just crossed our path.

After spending the night foraging, shortly after dawn hippopotamuses return to the river. These seemingly placid, comic-book-like characters who spend most of their lives submerged in water can move at thirty miles an hour and rip a human to pieces in seconds. Our entire schedule was predicated on waiting until their reentry before we traversed the river ourselves. A hippo seeking water is the most dangerous creature of Africa.

Now, ahead of us on the trail, the full-grown male hippopotamus had made his way back to the river without attacking us. My pounding heartbeat gradually slowed, and soon we were ready to cross the river—the same one full of crocodiles and hippos, including the giant beast we had just encountered.

We walked across the Tsavo River twice each day. We slept on the south bank, where a dirt track allowed our camps to be set up and food to be brought in from Nairobi every few days. We hiked along the roadless north bank on game trails where we were alone with the animals.

Our guides carefully chose a wide crossing normally frequented by elephants. We walked through mud toward thigh-high rushing water. Not only was it challenging, it was terrifying. We splashed noisily in a tight group, like a herd of elephants, nominally imitating those giant beasts—the only animals that both croc and hippo fear and avoid.

I would have splashed noisily even if no one had told

me to do so. On our first crossing, I stepped boldly into the water, almost immediately feeling my feet slipping downstream. I grabbed the sinewy black body next to me and held his arm in a death grip, as he tried to move me to the side away from his spear. It would be many crossings before I got the hang of it. This morning the river was higher than normal, quickly reaching above my waist due to the rain, leaving no room for bravado.

Crossing the river was the only time all day that we deliberately made noise. Sixty-five-year-old Mohammed, a tall, gaunt Samburu tribal leader who had walked this area for half a century, first as a game warden searching for poachers, now leading this unique expedition several times a year, instructed us to proceed silently. Our guides needed to hear every movement in the bush. We also had to walk in a single file, to prevent dangerous animals from cutting between us. It had to be straight, too, so that no one would come into the line of fire if shots became necessary.

I appreciated the rules more and more as the days went on. The quiet helped us merge more closely into the primeval world that surrounded us.

We walked through a dry and arid savanna, until, after seven dry months, the first rainfall made the land new and fresh. It was magical. A delicate mist bathed our skin, which had been covered for days with fine abrasive sand, like a beauty treatment gone awry. Patches of clear sky created just enough light and warmth to blanket the earth in translucent glowing voile.

Shortly after the rain began, a movement in some doum palms on our right caught my eye.

"There's a giraffe in the saltbush," whispered Alex.

NEVER A STRANGER

A delicate head atop a long neck paused to stare at us. I struggled to find words that would do justice to the living poetry surrounding me.

A short while later, seven elephants silently wandered across our path. After they passed by, unaware of our presence downwind, I stared for a long time at the lacy pattern left by their footpads. The delicate tracings on the damp soil transported me to a memory of my mother. She often stood at her bedroom window watching me come home from school, the open-weave lace curtain billowing around her, similarly patterned and as delicate as these footprints I now contemplated in the mist. My memory receded, and I wondered how 10,000 pounds of elephant could leave such a perfectly balanced imprint. Had it been fine China holding prime rib *au jus*, not a drop of liquid would have spilled, and the name Spode would have been clearly etched in the sand.

The tracks also reminded me of the young male elephant—nicknamed Brad, because he was so handsome—who had walked between our tents during the night. His step was delicate and quiet, only those still awake heard him, despite the fact that the only thing separating his massive body from ours was a thin canvas fabric. After, I waited as long as I could to step out and use the makeshift latrine dug in the sand. Brad was nowhere to be seen. Neither were any other members of our group. I savored the sense of fear and adventure of being the sole human under the southern night sky.

"Aaah, aaah... Ah, ah, ah, ah..."

The satisfied grunting of a male lion returned my attention to our walk. Starting long and then turning staccato, maybe a dozen altogether, the grunts were reminiscent of the call of a man, long married, reaching a familiarly satisfying apogee in the privacy of his bedroom. I waited in vain, however, for that long, final sigh, as we moved on.

Clouds gathered and the voile thickened to muslin. Drops spattered on my hat, then on the small notepad I scribbled on. My mind was flooded by so many impressions that I rushed to get them down in the moment, lest they be lost in the deluge of new sensations. Even still, I found that words could only begin to describe all the feelings that arose from walking through a land where the largest mammals on Earth still roam free.

Soil turned to mud. My feet got thick and heavy. Our footprints sank deeper, as did those of the elephants. I couldn't help but think how hard it must be for animals to move about in the rainy season. At least when there's more water, they have less need to move around. It was, in fact, due to the dry season that the animals were clustered around the river, making it possible for us to be here with them, however briefly.

The rain got serious. The ink on my paper started to run. I had to concentrate on walking for the final wet hours of the morning.

Mostly we walked in complete isolation. But the outside world did sometimes enter our awareness.

One day we saw tracks of poachers around a group of spooked elephants. One of our guides took off to report the situation to park wardens.

Another day the river took on a dark turquoise tinge that at first seemed beautiful but clearly was the sign of something unhealthy in the water. It disappeared a day later. We suspected a chemical spill far upriver.

And then, toward the end of our walk, we got news from the capital. The siege had ended. Sixty-seven were dead, and the police were accused of bungling the operation.

We finished our trip on the coast north of Mombasa and proceeded directly to Lamu, a small island on the Indian Ocean, an old Islamic community. That day, a Kenyan Muslim cleric was killed in Mombasa, sparking riots. Thankfully, during our visit Lamu was blessedly quiet—although it would fall victim to a terrorist attack a few months later.

The wild animals that most people fear when thinking about walking across Africa turned out not to be the biggest risk of our trip. It wasn't the animals, but man, who massacred elephants, spilled chemicals, blew up malls, and killed clerics in the two weeks we walked through a land preserved for the wild.

The wild went about its business, happy to be at a relatively safe distance from man's fearsome savagery.

27 NIRVANA IN A CUP

"You have to try egg coffee in Hanoi. It's delicious."

I looked up the best place to go and found Café Giang near my hotel. I wasn't a bloodhound on the trail, I confess; but I walked down the street and checked for the café where the address indicated. However, when I asked for number 39, one person pointed left, another pointed right. I got distracted by a group of men smoking a pipe made from a three-foot piece of bamboo. And then by women steering bicycles full of fruits and vegetables and endless commodities.

I never saw the café.

The next morning I decided to order an egg coffee at my hotel. I was staying at the Metropole, Hanoi's most famous hotel and one of its most sophisticated. Its guests have included Graham Greene, Charlie Chaplin, and my personal favorite, Joan Baez. Surely the hotel could handle an egg coffee.

The beautifully dressed young waitress was replaced by a gracious gentleman. He bowed and told me that, if I would wait six to eight minutes, he could bring me an egg coffee. When I asked if it took that long to make, he explained that he would have to find the place that makes them somewhere "in the garden."

Ten minutes later I was sipping my drink. The presentation was sublime. A delicately framed candle burned in a translucent porcelain base, which supported a larger square bowl half full of hot water. The coffee cup rested in the water. Every effort was made to keep it at the perfect temperature.

"How is it?" the waiter asked attentively.

"It is very nice." I graciously replied. Graciousness is my tactic when enthusiasm is lacking. The coffee tasted like the Three In One instant coffee I make in my room when traveling in Asia: cloyingly sweet hot liquid with the underlying taste of caffeine.

"You know," the man said, reading me perfectly, "I can tell you where to get a real egg coffee."

"Oh?"

"Yes, it is not far."

He walked to the front of the restaurant, grabbed a small notepad and pen, and wrote down: Giang Café, 39 Nguyen Huu Huan. My friend, Catherine, had also recommended this spot. So, it had to be.

This time I persevered. Fifteen minutes after I left the hotel, I scoured the side of the street where my map application sent me. Usually trustworthy, this time the app was way off. I crossed the road, walked up and down the other side of the block, and kept asking for number 39. Finally, someone spoke English and directed me almost next door, to a very narrow slot and then a stairway going up. I snapped a pic for future reference.

A group of Myanmar nuns I had been observing along the way followed me into the café. At tables that came to my knee, we sat down on chairs the height of a hiking boot.

After placing my order, I talked and laughed with the nuns, who were happy to meet someone who knew their country. Hugs were soon being exchanged, the nuns' joy expressed through requests for photographs—of me.

The café was reminiscent of a beatnik coffee shop in a rundown section of a large city. Mold competed with the paint on the walls. The furniture was something McDonald's should copy to get patrons out as quickly as possible. It would contort the average American into intolerable pain.

The egg coffee came in a simple cup with the café's logo. It rested in a small bowl of warm water. It looked like a small latte with a murky design. When stirred, the froth was dense. The liquid below was black.

And then, as I took my first sip, I was transported to my very earliest childhood. I closed my eyes and took one more sip of the coffee. Senses that hadn't been tantalized in decades burst to life.

I reached for my phone and sent a text to my brother. The tiny chair I now sat on matched the one my baby butt had cuddled as I waited impatiently for my mother to finish what she was doing. Holding a bowl in her hand, she beat its contents so hard, she threatened to destroy the bowl itself.

Gogglj-mogglj—the *j* making the ending baby-soft—was our name for these beaten egg yolks with sugar, gentled down to a creamy thickness by my mother's perfect touch. A tiny spoonful of it would roll through your mouth and line your throat with nirvana.

Egg coffee was apparently invented in Vietnam during difficult times when milk was hard to come by. My own Mama's treat had been made while we lived in a refugee camp with a similar dearth of ingredients.

I did a search on Google. It turned out that something called Kogel Mogel was created out of scarcity in Eastern Europe and is still eaten today by children in Poland. I've never asked my relatives in Serbia or Croatia about it, but I certainly will.

Hanoi and I have both moved far beyond our era of scarcity, but I have rediscovered a love affair with a token of gold that shined its light into my soul.

As I was leaving the café, I met the young man whose grandfather had opened it. The man pointed to his father, the baby in a portrait of the family. I will always remember Hanoi egg coffee as something his grandfather created for his father to keep him happy in hard times.

28 SEVEN O'CLOCK

"Why do I have to keep apologizing? Why do we Russians have to keep apologizing?"

I hear this while taking a walk in the woods. I am alone, taking a breather from the companionship of friends and family with whom I'm traveling in a remote area of Russia. I have slipped quietly out of the dacha, for everyone else is still asleep, recovering from a late night of conversation, food, and drink.

It is early May 2019. Much of Europe is blanketed in cold rain. Yet here, an hour east of Moscow, where it should be colder yet, the early morning sun is already warming the pine forests, and gentle mists are rising over wild grasses surrounding the many ponds in the area. A pair of hawks circles overhead, and a few black birds shout as if outraged, just like my crows at home.

Walking restores me. Doing so in the early morning, while life is still slow, lets me take in my surroundings without being overwhelmed. I often find myself talking to my phone, recording my impressions. Later, when I am home, I can reflect on and process the thoughts.

This is my last morning at *Zadneye Polye*, the small settlement where my friends' dacha is located. The previous morning, as I was heading back along empty roads to the house, a car appeared. A barking dog sped after it, followed by two middle-aged men on foot, one leading a heavy old bicycle. The men teased the dog about chasing wheels, then shared the joke with me. I didn't get it, but grinned and greeted them anyway.

The guy walking the bike, whose name was Evgenii, was drunk out of his mind. All the same, he seemed quite happy. He looked somewhere between an educated cosmopolitan and a vagrant—I couldn't quite place him. Clearly he'd had a long night.

I am just starting my walk now as Evgenii is heading home, this time alone. He is trying to ride the bike but gives up. He has obviously fallen, his legs covered with blood and dirt. But yesterday's smile is still there.

"Hello again," he says. "Where are you from?"

"I'm American."

"Oh." His eyes focus piercingly. He hadn't expected my answer. There aren't many American women wandering around his neighborhood, speaking his language.

"Did you buy a dacha here?"

"No, I'm visiting friends."

Rather than ask me more or, perhaps instead, stumble home, he gently asks, "Why do I have to keep apologizing? Why do we Russians have to keep apologizing?"

He says it like someone who feels horribly guilty but, at the same time, is tired of the burdens of the world landing on his shoulders.

"Why do I feel guilty about Ukraine? They were always our people."

Without waiting for a response, he continues.

"I wish people could all just love each other."

Learning that I am American has given him the opening. He moves to an extended commentary about how his country is being painted as the guilty party. He almost seems to forget about me as he searches within himself. Then he looks deep into my eyes.

"Are you Christian?" he asks.

"Yes, I am *pravoslavnaya*," I answer. The Russian word for the Orthodox faith literally means "true believer." Since it is the religion I was raised in, it's a safe answer.

"*Slava bogu*," thank the Lord, he says, relieved. He crosses himself in the Russian Orthodox manner, touching his right shoulder first.

It reminds me of the old Russian people I grew up with in San Francisco and the monastery we walked to on Saturday evenings. I knew that post-Soviet Russia had reverted to the religion Lenin had tried to eradicate, but I didn't expect to come across it on a walk in this remote countryside.

Evgenii and I move beyond religion, and he asks my age. I round up to seventy. A startled look comes in response, followed by a smile.

"You look so good I could jump in bed with you!" he exclaims.

It takes me a second to get what he means. I have not heard flirtation in Russian since I was a girl. Since he didn't say it in a lewd or unkind way, I take Evgenii's bold remark as a compliment.

He grins and continues. "You could be my mother," he says. "That's our generation gap. But you look so good, so upright, so confident. I could spend a lot of time with you."

His shoulders straighten, his smile grows wider, and the blood-stained vagrant morphs into a seductive Don Juan.

I am too astonished to say anything. It wouldn't matter anyway. Evgenii is on a roll and keeps talking until realizing that he's speaking in an informal way to a much older woman. A woman who could be his mother. This simply isn't done!

He apologizes—not for the comments, but for using the familiar you, *ti*, with me. He switches to the formal you, *vi*. He reiterates it's all meant as a sincere compliment.

Requiring little encouragement, Evgenii then goes off on a rambling, mostly one-sided conversation. He tells me about how his twenty-three-year-old grandfather fought and died in the battle of Minsk, one of the largest Russian victories in World War II. His other grandfather, who had two daughters, suffered a radically different fate.

"He earned some money and bought a bicycle," Evgenii says, pointing at his own bicycle. "They found it and accused him of earning money illegally. He was taken away by the NKVD, Stalin's secret police. He wrote once to his daughters from the gulag and said, 'I have lost my teeth. I cannot eat. I will soon die.'"

As Evgenii talks, I realize that his grandparents are the same generation as my father. He could have been describing the fate of my family, had they not fled the country in 1920. These are the sorts of stories I have come to Russia searching for. I don't yet understand that I will hear no others from a people so keen on guarding their privacy. Evgenii's intoxication has helped make him an exception.

Tearing up, he recounts that no one ever heard from his grandfather again. I touch Evgenii's shoulder and tell him he is a good man. And yet, as he looks at me again, I can see the responsibilities of being perceived by the world as the bad guy fall back on his shoulders. Now we are both near tears.

He continues, trying to talk about something more positive. He shares what he likes to do. At the moment, he is going to go home and watch the History channel, a program about the ancient Greeks. He is going to get his mind off all this horrible stuff.

"You know, it's only the Muslims we should be afraid of. I am afraid of that. I am terrified," he says.

Taken aback, I wonder if somewhere a Muslim is saying, "I am tired of being villainized. I just want everyone to be loved."

I keep reassuring Evgenii that he is a lovely man who has nothing to feel bad about. But my heart is breaking. He reaches out to shake my hand. And then he kisses it, wetting it with tears that won't stop.

"Goodbye, Zhenya," I say, switching to the less formal name he has asked me to call him.

He pushes his bicycle and stumbles on.

As I walk, I keep thinking about this young man, carrying on his shoulders the responsibility of his country's actions in the world; carrying them not just with the pride Putin works so hard to instill, but also with the shame felt from the rest of the world.

I feel ashamed of my country, of myself, of anyone who carries an attitude of their own righteousness with them as they travel through the world.

And it is only seven o'clock in the morning.

29 SEVILLA FAREWELL

I stepped out the door of the Hotel Imperial, onto the same ragged lane I had found almost depressing on my arrival two weeks earlier. But now the scene glowed with warm memories, friendship, and the imprint of Spanish two-cheek kisses and American hugs. The previous days and nights had been a feast of tasty tapas and *Semana Santa* processions with giant Jesus floats led by towering Klan-like coneheads. It was difficult to be leaving with Easter approaching.

As my taxi driver took my luggage and opened the door, I heard high heels clicking on the polished stones of the passage. I turned and caught sight of eyes gleaming beneath the black lace of a mantilla. I couldn't stop staring.

The young woman paused her conversation with her partner, and we did the two-step required to share the narrow street.

"Oh my god," I breathed. "You are beautiful!"

They didn't speak English, but the couple got the point. They stopped and, in my broken Spanish, I learned that from now until Easter this was how most of the women of

Seville would be dressing.

I touched the woman's arms, unable to decide if they were covered in tattoos or lace. Then I asked if I could take her picture. As she started to pose for the camera, my taxi driver came around and insisted I should be in the photo, too.

The woman and I chatted away until the taxi driver tapped his watch and pointed helplessly at the cars lined up behind him.

"The streets might be full of women in black," I said,

"but you are my first. What a gift. Thank you, thank you."

And then she practiced her English.

"You made my day!" she exclaimed, her smile widening.

We hugged in farewell, whereupon I realized I had been ignoring her partner, a handsome young man in inconspicuous street attire. I apologized for excluding him—but was blunt: he just couldn't compete with his beautiful girlfriend.

He laughed, we hugged, and I jumped into the taxi.

30 DO YOU REMEMBER ME?

"Hello, my friend. Do you remember me?"

I looked up as a donkey jostled the stranger approaching me in the square of the small town. He deftly sidestepped to avoid the dung the animal was plopping on the worn stone.

A vague memory flickered, and I felt a smile starting. But my days with the slick touts in the souk of Marrakesh—where I had started this trip to Morocco—had toughened me up.

I had learned through repeated miscalculations that in the souk "Hello again!" is one of the most common tactics used by relentless shopkeepers. An instinctive politeness makes you respond—assuming this is a person you have met. And then you are doomed. Doomed. You are lured into looking at a profusion of pottery, a superfluity of scarves, an alphabet soup of spices, rugs for countless palaces, jewels to adorn harems. Babouches! Djellabas! Kaftans! A plethora of pastiche in a complex, meandering maze.

It couldn't be starting again. Surely I had left this

intrusive, intense, and relentless pursuit of my dollars behind?

I was spending a few days in the northern hill town of Moulay Idriss, a holy place where Islam was first introduced to Morocco many centuries ago. It felt like a place of calm, beyond the chaos. I was readjusting to people who wanted no more than recognition in return for their welcome.

I stopped and looked more closely at this man. He returned my gaze expectantly.

Just a few hours earlier I had explored nearby Volubilis, a spectacular Roman ruin in the countryside. Ready to head back to my hotel, I was pleased to find a local taxi outside the ruins. The driver waved me toward the back door of the old car. I opened the door, only to wish I hadn't: it was crowded with bodies—male bodies.

Swarthy young men lowered their eyes. It was the only car available, and the driver was getting restless. I jumped in, the men shifted to make room, and the taxi lurched off, stopping suddenly as a hand pounded on the window. Space was made for one more passenger, who nimbly leaped toward the back, then almost tripped as his eyes met mine.

"*Salaam alaichum*," he said, the traditional Arabic greeting meaning "peace be upon you."

"*D'où venez-vous?*" he added, after righting himself.

We were on a dirt road heading toward town. The guy next to me was muttering on his phone, and—other than furtive glances confirming the unexpected nature of my presence—until then everyone had pretended to ignore me. They were just as surprised to be joined by a foreigner the age of their grandmothers as I had been to realize the taxi was a shared one.

"*De la Californie*," I replied.

"*Ah,*" he continued, "*et que pensez-vous du Maroc?*"

What did I think of Morocco? All eyes fastened onto me, even the driver's, in the rearview mirror.

"*Je l'aime beaucoup! Les gens sont très gentils!*" I answered, confirming my love for his country and the kindness of its people.

"*Merci, merci,*" he thanked me, before translating my reply for the others. Tensions eased, and Mohammed—as he introduced himself—told me how happy they all were that I had chosen their country to visit.

Mohammed switched from French—the second language of the country—to the more challenging English, explaining that he worked as a history teacher in a neighboring village.

We pulled over for yet another passenger whose "*salaam*" stretched and faded into "*alaaaiiiiichum...*" as he stared at me. When he smiled, I offered my hand. Soon everyone was shaking it, some forgetting to let go. Men holding an unknown woman's hand was clearly something unusual here.

"This was Morocco's first city," Mohammed started. But before going any further, he shouted an urgent "stop" and jumped out. He bowed to me before parting, tossing a coin to the driver. I got out soon after.

Now, some hours later, I did remember him.

"Of course! So good to see you again."

He smiled and nodded, continuing on his way after wishing me a good visit.

Warmed by the unexpected encounter with Mohammed, I continued my walk around town. I passed the street stand where I had eaten tagine with friends the night before. The chef, Abdo, had uncovered several gorgeous peaks of vegetables artistically layered in now-familiar clay dishes with conical tops—they, too, called "tagines." After, he insisted I pose with him for a photo.

Further on, I met a young woman herding some children along a blue alley.

"*C'est Fatima*," she said with a laugh, indicating the daughter now hanging onto my hand as if it were a rare gift. "*Et je m'appelle Zora.*"

"*Ce n'est pas possible!*" I exclaimed.

I am not sure the woman understood when I explained that she shared my mother's name; but, once I taught her five-year-old son to use my phone, we huddled for a family portrait—with the American.

When I stopped to take a picture of a donkey munching some greens in the countryside, a young lad jumped on its back and stood up to make the picture more interesting. When I sat on a cement ledge next to a mosque, a shoeshiner handed me a seat cushion, warming my heart almost as much as my bottom. Later, when I passed a girl in a doorway and blew her a kiss, her mother gaily shouted *"bisou!"* She then brought another infant barreling from behind the door and into my arms. We laughed as we spun in circles.

On my arrival a day earlier, I had approached Moulay Idriss alone and on foot. It was my second visit, so I wasn't worried about getting lost. The road weaved through olive groves, and sheep cleared the growth between trees, fertilizing and weed-whacking the old-fashioned way.

As I walked, a group of young men materialized around me, slowing to match my pace. I slowed further. So did they. Was I mad to be out here alone?

Any momentary concerns were allayed as, rather than to an attack, I fell victim to the men's persistent charm. One of them spoke French, another some English. They serenaded me, accompanied by metal double castanets—called a *qraqeb*—which they tried to teach me to play. We walked and sang, the leader calling out the key word, the rest of us intoning in response. I had no idea what we were singing, but there was joy and laughter and music. Time flew.

Eventually we passed four young women who slowed and stared at me. I paused, worried that the guys were singing something embarrassing; that they were perhaps laughing *at* me, rather than *with* me. But a girl who understood my French confirmed they were, indeed, singing nicely. The two groups smiled at each other, tentatively.

When we moved on, I learned that earlier the men had been snubbed by the same group of women. The girls were

Berber, the boys Arab. They suspected this as the cause, although one explained that his mother, too, was Berber. Now that they had a rather unusual chaperone, a door seemed to have opened. I was thrilled that my presence could possibly help the two groups to connect with each other.

We approached town, posing for photos for one last time before parting. Idriss, who studied computer science, asked me to send him a group picture. I noted his email address, then shook hands with each of the young men, knowing they were reluctant to let me go.

"*Tu es la première Américaine que j'ai jamais touchée*," the last one said, clasping my arm. Perhaps he had dreamed that the first American woman he touched would be a seductive beauty, someone more akin to whom he might have encountered if he had met me many years earlier. All the same, the young Moroccan looked me in the eye and smiled warmly, touching me that much more deeply.

All too soon, my trip was over.

Back in America the news poured out in a relentless flood, the media hawking their points of view like touts in a global souk. A brute in the White House. Rising global tensions. The radical Islam of ISIS. Hatred and horror, anger and fear.

Taking a break from the ugliness, I looked at photographs from my trip. A town on a hill glows in otherworldly light. A kid standing on a donkey grins. The beauty of vegetable tagines complements Abdo's smile. Zora leans close while her children fuss. And eight slightly scruffy youths look both shy and protective at the same time.

I might not recognize these young men if I encountered them again on the street, just as at first I hadn't recognized Mohammed. But I was now Facebook friends with Abdo and Idriss, so I posted pictures and video of our encounters. I loved seeing the comments from their friends and mine. One translated as "Gratitude from the official sponsor of tourism for Moulay Idriss": كبور الراعي الرسمي للسياحة بمولاي ادريس زرهون. Others marveled at what their world looked like through my eyes.

In response to my post of our songfest, Idriss wrote, "I will never forget this moment." As tears I don't even try to hold back attest, neither will I.

Yes, my friends, I certainly do remember you.

I do remember you.

ABOUT THE AUTHOR

Tania Romanov Amochaev is an award-winning travel photographer and author of *Mother Tongue: A Saga of Three Generations of Balkan Women*. A Solas Award winner, Tania's work has been featured in multiple travel anthologies, including the *Best Travel Writing* series. Born in the former Yugoslavia, Tania fled the country and spent her childhood in a refugee camp in Trieste, Italy, before emigrating to the United States. She hasn't stopped traveling since.

taniaromanov.com

www.ingramcontent.com/pod-product-compliance
Lightning Source LLC
Chambersburg PA
CBHW020418010526
44118CB00010B/314